Common Weal
All Of Us First

Published by Scottish Left Review Press
for the Jimmy Reid Foundation, June 2014.
ISBN 978-0-9550362-7-9

Printed and Bound in Great Britain by
Thomson the Printers, 14 Carnoustie Place,
Glasgow G5 8PB.

All the credit for this work belongs with the
many contributors who authored the reports
on which it is based. All the blame for the
presentation of this work belongs with its
editor, Robin McAlpine.

With many thanks to Tangent for the
wonderful design work on this book.
www.tangentgraphic.co.uk

Prologue

Scotland's people are in a unique position - we have been invited to imagine our nation afresh. So let's do it. Let us ask what our country would look like if we were to design it now. Twelve months ago this is what the Jimmy Reid Foundation did. It began work that became known as the 'Common Weal project'. It started with simple aims - let's think about what we want to achieve, let's look around the world to see who has achieved it, let's examine how they achieved it and let's learn the lessons and apply them to 21st Century Scotland.

As the project got under way person after person, team after team came forward offering their expertise. In those twelve months the project snowballed. It now consists of over 50 major policy reports by scores of authors on everything from tax and banking to arts and food to industry and work to democracy and land. Together they build up a carefully-constructed, heavily-researched, well-referenced and compellingly-argued case for the transformation of Scotland. This is arguably the single biggest reimagining of a nation state in modern history.

But who can read 50 academic reports? Common Weal is about creating a politics and a society which once again puts citizens at its heart, so if it excluded them on the basis of complexity and jargon it would be hypocritical. A politics that can change Scotland can only be a politics that includes everyone.

So in these pages is an attempt to bring together the content of 50 major reports as a single programme for action. But with self-imposed rules - no jargon, no bullet-points, no footnotes, no graphs and charts, no itallics, no language that could not be understood by any school-leaver. If you want these things they are in the reports; these pages are almost in an oral tradition, a story that takes us from the nation we are to the nation we can be.

Of course, in all these many pages of policy work there will be ideas and proposals that not everyone will precisely agree with and there will be other issues people feel are missing or insufficiently covered. But they do offer a consistent approach, a coherent philosophy - and a genuine path to a different future.

All of this takes place in the context of a debate about whether Scotland should become an independent country. This is not meant to be a case for or a case against independence but only a case for a better Scotland. Many of the authors involved believe that change can only come if Scotland takes the powers in its own hands – but some do not. What unites everyone who has been involved in this project is the belief that this must be an agenda for Scotland's future no matter what the outcome of the referendum.

Scotland cannot go back to accepting the nation it is just now. Inequality, poverty, declining infrastructure, powerless communities, closed politics, profiteering, low pay, overwork, anxiety, stress and unhappiness – it is time to end the myth that we will ever defeat these problems unless we act decisively.

What's stopping us? It's certainly neither the desire for change nor the wealth and resources needed to make that change. Until now the biggest barrier has been confidence – we have been trained to believe that no alternative is possible, that achieving a decent society is just too damn complicated, so best not to try.

In these pages you will see that change isn't complicated, it just requires will and hard work. The idea that in Scotland there just isn't the savvy to drag ourselves up is nonsense. The idea that it can't be done is disproved by all the other nations who have done it. And the clever-clever arguments that suggest there is something about Scotland that means we can't do what they did? You can choose to believe them, but you will need to resign yourself to failure and decline.

By the time you reach the last of these pages you will know exactly how Scotland can be changed. You will have the knowledge to explain how it can be done. You will have the confidence that everything in these pages has been tried somewhere and shown to work. You will be able to explain how it can be paid for. Hopefully you will have the confidence to believe this can be our future.

What will happen next? No-one knows. But all across Scotland people are waking up. They are rubbing their eyes, remembering that this is their country and becoming angry at what it has become. If they too can have the knowledge of how we can change and the confidence that we can do it, for how much longer can the elite run our lives without our consent. The elite may spend their wealth persuading us that this is as good as it gets. Thankfully, democracy is more powerful again than they are.

We – the people of Scotland – have the power to build a Common Weal Scotland. First, let's look at how we can do it. All of the reports can be found at www.reidfoundation.org and on allofusfirst.org where there is ongoing discussion of Common Weal.

Chapter One

A NEW POLITICS

We've had 40 years of Me First politics – and we all came second. It is time for a politics that puts All Of Us First

Let us imagine a Scotland that begins from the hopes of its citizens. What are those hopes?

To have a secure, affordable home in a community where you can enjoy going outside to a clean and healthy environment. To be healthy and to feel good. To know you'll have enough money to pay the bills and to buy what you need and to know that you'll have that financial security in the future. To have meaningful, secure, satisfying work that you care about. To have good relationships with family and friends and to know those you care about are safe and secure. To be part of a community and to know that the other members of that community are also cared for, safe and secure. To have access to green and wild spaces, community spaces and play areas; to arts, hobbies and leisure activities; to good transport links. To have good facilities and high-quality services locally when you need them. To have our human rights, to be free from discrimination, to be accepted and respected. To live a good life.

Home, work, security, community, recreation, public service and respect; a politics which cares about us would be built on these foundations. Profiteering, competition, elitism, greed, anger, blame and mistrust are not words that represent our hopes. So why are they the foundations of the politics we have?

Me-First politics persuaded us that if we let the strongest get stronger, the biggest get bigger and the richest become richer we'd all benefit because some of their wealth and power would 'trickle down' to us. It didn't. The bigger corporations got, the richer the rich became, the more they found ways to make sure that the rest of us didn't get any share. The argument that through conflict we sort out the 'winners' from the 'losers' and that this is good for all of us has no credibility left; be it tax-dodging billionaires, profiteering energy companies or criminal banks, it was a blank cheque for cheats and bullies.

The Me-First politics of conflict have set us all against each other. Worker, small business owner, pensioner, student, mother, immigrant, the disabled, the poor – whomever we are we're meant to blame all our problems on someone else who is like us but a bit different. This is no future for Scotland. We don't need blame, we don't need resentment, we don't need anger. We need change.

Common Weal is an old Scots phrase that means both 'wealth shared in common' and 'for the wellbeing of all'. It has become the name for a different kind of politics, a politics that puts All Of Us First. It is a politics that begins from what we say we want for our lives, not from what an elite tells us we are allowed or not allowed. It is a politics that begins from a belief that we can build more and reach higher when we work together than we can when we work against each other.

All-Of-Us-First politics believe that we all get better social and economic outcomes when we behave in a mutual way. This means we start not by focussing on the small number of things that divide us but on the much larger number of things that bring us together. Success will come when we can 'coincide' the interests of different groups, seeking ways of doing things that help not one against the other but both at the same time.

This is not soft idealism but a hard-headed analysis of the world we live in. Countries like Britain which have pursued a conflict model of economic and social development over the past thirty years have been worst at living up to the hopes of their citizens. Even more damningly, they have been worst at achieving economic success, the measure by which they would have themselves judged.

By comparison, countries like Denmark, Sweden, Norway or Finland which pursue a more mutual model of social and economic development top all the world's charts on meeting the hopes of their citizens. Even more impressively they out-perform the Me-First nations across virtually all measures of economic success.

The Common Weal project is based on 50 major reports that look at subjects from housing to tax, sport to the economy, health to transport, energy to the environment. Every one of these reports has looked around the world to find out who has achieved the best results in each field, not so we can copy them but so we can learn from them.

The reports learn the lessons and then ask what it would look like if we applied those lessons to Scotland today. Everything that is proposed in these reports has been tried somewhere else – and shown to work. In every case the cost of proposals and where the money will come from has been explained. This is a hard-headed assessment of who has done better than us, why they've done better and what we can learn. It has been produced by scores of leading academics, economists and thinkers. It stands as a realistic and achievable alternative to Me-First politics.

So how do we build a Scotland that puts All Of Us First? At the heart of Common Weal is work. Me-First politics would have you believe that

Common Weal is an old Scots phrase that means both
'wealth shared in common' and 'for the wellbeing
of all'. It has become the name for a different kind of
politics, a politics that puts All Of Us First.

it is big business profits that makes us all wealthier. In fact, Me-First economics sees big business profits and economic growth as the same thing.
The reality is very different – the people of Britain have got poorer as big
business has got richer. This kind of economic growth is actually making us
worse off.

So what does make us wealthier? Work. When work is working it
increases our wages and gives us security. When work is working a greater
share of national wealth is paid in wages. When work is working higher wages
mean people pay their taxes and don't need benefits. When work is working
it creates good public finances which can be invested in public facilities and
services. When work is working it focuses on working better, not working
longer – which gives us time to participate in family life, community life and
society. When work is working we feel involved in our work and feel treated
with respect.

When work is working our lives get better; when work is failing we
get poorer and unhappier, more tired, more stressed, more anxious. It is work
that matters most, not just profit.

Of course, whether we can create good work depends on the economy – but it doesn't just depend on how big it is, it depends on how good it is.
If an economy is growing by creating more and more low-pay jobs it simply
makes us all poorer – the low-pay worker is poorer because they need benefits, the higher-pay worker is poorer because they have to pay for benefits.
Only low-pay big business grows richer.

A Me-First economy is designed to promote and support businesses
that can extract the maximum wealth from the economy in the shortest possible time while making the minimum possible investment. This is what profit
has come to mean – most extracted with least invested in the shortest time
possible. The outcome is low-pay jobs in high-volume sectors which make

their profits not from the skills of their employees but from taking as much out of the pockets of their customers as they can. They don't build things, make things, change things or do things – they mark up prices, inflate costs, monopolise markets, fleece customers, crush smaller competitors and exploit their suppliers. Letting financial service companies steal from their customers, letting energy companies endlessly increase their prices, letting big supermarkets close down our high streets and impoverish our farmers, letting property speculators grow rich from rising house prices which leave young families struggling to make ends meet – this is what Me-First politics calls 'economic growth'. And we're told there is nothing we can do about it because this is the 'law of the market', a law we must accept in silence.

By contrast, a Common Weal economy is designed to promote and support the enterprises that can create the maximum value for the long term through the skills of their workforce and by investing to improve. What will make us successful is how much value an employee adds in each hour they work as a result of their skills and the business's investment in infrastructure and innovation – all of which is called productivity. The more productive a worker is, the more value they add to a business. The more value a worker adds to a business, the higher the wages they will receive. The more productive the economy as a whole, the more capacity it has to increase the wealth of citizens. The more productive a business becomes as a result of skills, investment and innovation the stronger and more secure is the future of that business.

Making things, building things, creating things, inventing things, doing complex things well, doing simple things better; this is what creates real wealth and good jobs. Almost everyone accepts that our economy has to be rebalanced in this way, if for no other reason than to reduce the vulnerability of relying on a small number of industries. It's just that Me-First politics does not believe we should try because it does not believe we should interfere in the interests of big business. So it crosses its fingers and hopes that big business will be less selfish for a while. And it never happens.

In a Common Weal Scotland we would see the economy as part of society and not the other way around. And since we live in a democratic society that means we have a democratic right to express a view on the nature of our economy. If Scotland's citizens want a high-pay economy then our democracy must respond. Which means we must accept that there is no such thing as 'neutrality' – everything a government does favours one kind of economy or another. We just have to stop favouring a low-pay, exploitative economy and start favouring a high-pay, productive one.

A democratic national attempt to favour a better, more productive economy by using the full range of government powers is called an industrial policy. It was an industrial policy that created the most impressive period of sustained economic improvement in Britain's history and it is an industrial policy that helps keep other successful economies innovative and productive. We need many more Scottish businesses, many more manufacturing business-es, much more variation in kinds of business (private companies, cooperatives, mutuals and so on), many more sizes of business and a much more integrated economy where businesses are used to working together. And we need to build that economy based on one thing – our wealth. The wealth of skills of our people, the wealth of natural resources of our nation, the wealth of the infrastructure we build.

So we have to make a choice – the All-Of-Us-First strategy of having an industrial policy to create change or the Me-First strategy of crossing our fingers and hoping it will be OK.

The Me-First obsession with 'magic buttons' that you can press that will, in one stroke, solve all our problems has been found out to be rubbish. The one thing that matters isn't deregulation. The one thing that matters isn't low regulation. The one thing that matters isn't low tax. The one thing that matters is everything we do. When people say that social problems are 'too complex to fix', they really mean 'too complicated to fix with one easy answer'. There isn't one answer.

So if we can succeed in implementing an industrial policy based on the work of our people and resources of our nation it is the first step to cre-ating a high-pay economy – but we will need many more steps. We need a welfare policy that emphasises not fear and anxiety to scare people out of poverty but 'social security' that gives people the assurance and self-belief to build a life for themselves.

We need proper industrial democracy so that workers can be empow-ered to shape their working lives and employers can learn from their workers experience. We need a childcare policy that helps women into work. We need a national investment strategy that ploughs much-needed investment into the economy, our communities and our infrastructure. We need a housing strategy

Every citizen must face the fact that there is no-one coming to rescue us. It is up to us. A future built with our hands or a future built without us.

that turns homes into affordable, secure places to live not 'investment opportunities' for people with 'property portfolios'.

This will all create a foundation on which to build that better Scotland. As we move towards the strong public finances that come from a high-pay economy we can start to tackle the problems in our society. First among them are poverty and inequality. A high-pay economy based on productivity and industrial democracy tackles both head-on.

But we must do more. Whenever we create public policy based on putting people on different sides, it is always the side with less power that loses out – the poor or the disabled or women or ethnic minorities. If we create public services which are only for the poor and exclude everyone else, other people don't have a vested interest in making sure they are great services. And great services is what people who face poverty really need. Targeting, means-testing or any other system which makes the poor stand apart from everyone else will fail them. Any time in recent history where policies have improved the lives of the poor they have been policies that benefited everyone – like the NHS. When everyone cares, everyone benefits – and when everyone benefits its the poor that benefit most. This is called universalism and it has improved the lives of the least well off in a way that rationed, means-tested and marketised public services never have.

But it's not just the poor who need a better Scotland – we all do. Below the level of the Scottish Parliament, Scotland is one of the least democratic and most centralised countries in the developed world. We have enormous, distant local authorities that manage people's communities without involving them – and often without listening to them. Other than in elections, citizens have almost no say in how their country or community is run and opportunities to participate in democracy in any meaningful way are few and far between.

Commercial power and the power of vested interest has only one counterbalance – democracy. And since commercial power has never been stronger it is a great worry that belief in our democratic institutions has never been weaker. The 'stand still while we fix you' attitude of public policy administrators must come to an end. It is time that we trusted ourselves to make our own decisions – workers in the workplace, residents in our communities, citizens in our nation. Wealthy professionals in big, distant organisations using their 'expertise' to manage our lives without consulting us cannot be the future. We need to re-democratise Scotland.

Then we must look at our collective wealth and use it more effectively. Fairer taxes and a coherent approach to budgeting that eradicates the self-defeating policy of austerity and borrows to invest will share and use our national wealth more effectively. Then we must make sure that things people can't live without are not used to strip them of their own wealth and wellbeing – some things like energy and transport should be mainly owned by the people for the people and others like food and housing must be managed in a way that promotes wellbeing first and corporate profit a distant second. Our natural resources – our land, sea, wind, tide, fishing, oil – must be managed in a way that benefits everyone and not just the biggest corporations. The more people to whom we give a chance to build from the resources we have, the more will be built. And we must protect, grow and give everyone access to our environmental and cultural wealth as well.

Because a politics which says 'we're here to promote profit – the quality of your life is your own problem' is not a politics fit for Scotland. Participating in society, community and culture, being free from stress and anxiety, having time with your family and friends, having access to facilities and healthy, positive spaces – these are the things that make a good life. So public policy that harms these things is the politics of misery. Forcing us into long working hours, leaving us in fear of losing our jobs, taking away local libraries, leaving us no time or money to participate – all of this is preventing a good life. A good life is political and if politics washes its hands of its responsibility to give us a fighting chance of a good life then we need to wash our hands of that politics.

If we measure only how big things have got without measuring how good they have become we create a nation of giant mediocrity (if we're lucky...). If we measure ourselves only according to how those at the top are doing then we create a nation fit only for those at the top. And if we ignore the things that people say matter to them because they are things that don't matter to big business, we create a nation that is not fit for its citizens.

A Common Weal Scotland is a Scotland fit for its citizens. A Scotland built on a foundation of what matters to us, using our collective wealth to create the kinds of lives we say we want to live. It begins with a politics that cares about us and our hopes, not just our obedience and our votes.

So as you read through the many ideas and solutions that will build that Common Weal Scotland, you will find the same themes coming up over and over, a series of threads that tie together all of the work of Common Weal.

Shared interests create shared success – mutualism, universalism, equality and togetherness make things better for us all.

Strength comes from balance – relying on too much on a few things has made us vulnerable.

We make better decisions together – decisions that affect people must be made by the people they affect.

To build more we must share more – the more resources we can put in the most hands, the more we will create and the more successful we will become.

Investment is hope – we expend time, effort and resource now in the belief it will create a better future.

Design for life – if we want citizens to have a good life we need to design our society so they have a fighting chance.

All that matters is everything we do – 'magic' solutions and quick answers don't work. Only patience, commitment, coordination and hard work.

Changing not blaming – we can use our hands to point the finger or we can use our hands to build. But not both at the same time.

Some people say that you can't have a Common Weal Scotland in a world-wide Me-First economy. They seem to think that if we can't create utopia then there is no point in trying to be better. But Denmark, Sweden, Finland and Norway all exist in a Me-First world and have managed to put all of their people first in a way we can barely imagine.

Some people say that you can't have a Common Weal Scotland because there are 'rules' that won't let you. But other countries work within the same rules and they've done much better than us.

Some people say that you can't have a Common Weal Scotland because we have a history and tradition of a Me-First society. But histories and traditions are changed by the will of people, and the will for change is found everywhere in today's Scotland.

This is not a time for people who have lost their nerve but for people who are brave, committed and ready to work for change. This is not a time we can afford to waste talking endlessly about what we can't do but to talk about what we can do. This is not a time to knock things down but to build them up.

In Scotland we have more than enough vision and skill to change our nation. We have all the resources we need to make that change. We have a clear explanation of how can be done. And we have a very large democratic demand for change.

Scotland is a society with the tools, the wealth, the knowledge and the will to become a nation that puts all of its people first. It is our generation which will pick up those tools, invest that wealth, use that knowledge and harness that will. Or it is our generation which will squander it.

Every citizen must face the fact that there is no-one coming to rescue us. It is up to us. A future built with our hands or a future built without us. Whatever happens, this is our choice.

Chapter Two

A PEOPLE'S NATION

Participatory democracy means our nation can be run
by its people, for its people

Put power in the hands of communities with proper
local democracy.

Put power in the hands of ordinary people with
open, inclusive government.

Invest in our citizens.

Build from a foundation of human rights.

Invest in a democratic media.

Use clear language and communicate to inspire.

A better Scotland begins with democracy.

The State should be nothing more than an agreement between its citizens. Citizens choose a government to do the things that can only be done by pooling our resources and working together and to create and enforce laws. A government should have power only to the extent that the people have granted it and should have legitimacy in direct proportion to how well it is carrying out what was promised. We often call this agreement between citizens the 'social contract', the often unspoken deal which means we all recognise the need to give a little and take a little if we want to create a society worth living in.

When citizens vote in an election they should not be handing over a blank cheque and they are certainly not crowning an absolute ruler. The state is not supposed to be an army of unelected 'professionals' and 'experts' governing by decree; it is not supposed to be an agreement between multinational corporations and a ruling elite. That this is how it sometimes feels reveals something important; there is more than one kind of democracy.

Democracy is a system which lets the citizens of a nation decide how that nation is run, what it does, how it behaves. A representative democracy works by letting you vote for politicians once every four or five years; in between times they are only subject to the criticism of civil society, the media and their peers. A participatory democracy does of course have elected politicians but it also has many ways for ordinary people to participate in decision-making all the time. It designs its democracy to have the maximum opportunities for people to get involved in standing for election, whether they are in a political party or not. It brings democracy as close to the people who are affected by decisions as is possible. When decisions have to be made it involves the public in making and shaping those decisions. It is an attempt to create government by participation – where those affected by decisions are involved in the making of the decision.

Scotland is certainly not a participatory democracy. In fact, in terms of creating a democracy that enables people to get involved in elected politics, Scotland probably has the worst track record in the developed world. Every time there is a local election in Finland, one out of every 140 people stands for election. In Norway it's one in 81, in Sweden one in 145, in an average part of Germany one in 141. In Scotland it is one in 2,071. In these other countries between 3.6 and 5.5 candidates contest each available seat – there is real choice and real competition. In Scotland only 2.1 candidates contest each available seat. Which is to say that in the last local elections in Scotland almost half of everyone who stood got elected, almost as if we'd just tossed a coin.

We also have by far the least 'local' politics in the developed world. The average population of a local authority area in Europe is 5,620. In Scotland it is 163,000 – our local authorities are nearly 30 times bigger than average. The average physical size of a European local authority is 49 square kilometres; the average size of a Scottish local authority is 2,461 square kilometres, more than 50 times bigger. Even a country like Denmark, which has a lot of sparsely populated areas like Scotland, manages an average local authority size of 440 square kilometres. In fact, Scotland has one local authority that has a land area bigger than Belgium. How is that local? How is any of this local?

Scotland's local democracy is certainly not local and in many ways it is barely democratic. There is hardly a community in Scotland which is allowed to make a single significant decision for itself – at best they can send one councillor to a giant local authority which is possibly dozens of miles away and then keep their fingers crossed. More often than not the local authority will just let unelected 'experts' make the decision. Compare this with a close neighbour; in Norway a level of government we would call community council holds the budget and policy responsibility for their local hospital. Local communities control their local healthcare and can shape it to their local needs. In Scotland it is much more likely that a commercial consultancy report written by a global firm of accountants will decide what level of local healthcare you are permitted.

This is a national scandal. How can we possibly tolerate a system that seems to treat its citizens as incapable of making decisions about their own communities? How long can people put up with their towns and their neighbourhoods being run with little or no reference to what they themselves say they need and want? What confidence can we have in authorities which sit between the national and local media, held sufficiently to account by neither? How can we feel good about local governance most of which happens behind closed doors, often between big businesses and unelected officials? Or about democracy that keeps setting up secret, private organisations (such as the so-called Arms Length Executive Organisations) and then running democratically-funded services via these closed-shops where councillors can appoint themselves and their contacts? Scotland's rebirth will begin when democracy stops treating our citizens as if they are children that must be looked after in case they make the 'wrong' decision.

Until Scotland's people are allowed to make their own decisions for their own communities we will not be a mature democracy. And sometimes that means that communities will make bad decisions, just like the professional class make bad decisions. But since a local community will actually have to live with any bad decisions they make, unlike the professional class they might be expected to learn from the experience.

We need a real local democracy. This means another layer of elected local authorities which actually represent the communities in which people live. These will vary greatly in size – some might be the size of a village, some might be the size of a large town. But they must have real power and proper budgets to deal with issues such as the provision of local childcare, local transport, the running of local facilities, local planning decisions, the management of local schools, building up the local economy, promoting local tourism and so on. All of this must be done within national frameworks of quality, standards and principles so that no matter where you live you will always have a guarantee of strong, universal public services. But we have to stop being afraid of different communities making different choices. That is what local democracy should mean.

This does not require an expensive upheaval of our current local authority bureaucracies. All that has to happen is that rather than those

Much of what has gone wrong with democracy stems from a breakdown of trust between state and individual and that lack of trust has infected our other relationships.

bureaucracies taking instructions from one elected body it takes instruction on different issues from different elected bodies. For example, the existing councils might continue to set policy for business development services whereas the new local authorities might set policy for the design and build of its local school. Gradually more staff should be dispersed from the centralised authorities towards the genuinely local authorities. The set-up costs of this new system would be minimal and since the people who stand for elections in their communities will not be paid, the running costs will also be minimal.

Creating genuine local democracy will do no more than bring Scotland up to the standards of a normal developed country. That isn't far enough. If we want a really participatory democracy we need to change our attitudes to how we 'do' government.

At the moment two of the fundamental principles of democracy in Scotland appear to be 'government by expert' and 'management of the public'. Many of Scotland's most important institutions are run, not by any representative or democratic body but almost wholly, by bodies of people who have been privately appointed. And the vast majority of those appointed are older and come from the richest ten per cent of society – with the same wealthy individuals to be found running more than one organisation.

Then when governments either want to make a controversial decision (or want to justify a controversial decision they've already made) they set up an 'expert group', a class of people who appear again and again in positions of unelected power and are almost wholly drawn from the wealthiest five per cent of the population. Making decisions in committees where everyone comes from the same kind of background and thinks the same kinds of things is a recipe for 'group think' – if no-one is willing to challenge a bad idea or a wrong assumption, bad ideas become 'good' and wrong assumptions become 'true'. That is why not a single government advisor doubted there were weapons of mass destruction in Iraq or spotted the financial crisis coming. Worst of all, people who do seek to challenge the prevailing 'group think' are often excluded from decision-making for that very reason.

If 'group think' produces proposals that the public do not agree with (such as the privatisation of the Royal Mail), the public is seen as a 'problem' that has to be 'managed'. This is why the public is often not consulted until a decision is nearly made, with the wider public only being asked how something should be done, not whether it should be done in the first place.

Now of course we must draw on the expertise of people who have spent their lives learning about a subject and who are willing to give up their time for the public good. But making good decisions is about more than facts. For example, it is factually correct that if we closed all accident and emergency wards between two o'clock and six o'clock in the morning (times when there are fewer accidents), hospitals would automatically become 'more efficient'. But that won't help you if you have an accident at three o'clock in the morning. The right decision should always balance different facts, but should be driven by what citizens want from their government.

All of these bad practices can be changed; there are tried and tested alternatives for all of them.

First, in most occasions there is no need to appoint people to run big institutions without any democratic mandate. Usually it is possible to identify a 'community' of people who are directly interested in or affected by big institutions and it is perfectly possible to let them select the people that run those institutions democratically. For example, students, academics and staff can elect the people who sit on university courts (which make all the decisions about how a university is run, how much senior staff are paid, what priorities the university should invest in and so on). In other cases it would be possible to create communities, for example by allowing practising artists to register and then vote for who runs Creative Scotland, the agency that funds the arts in Scotland. Patronage is a medieval process in which powerful people divide up power between themselves. It is not democracy.

Second, there is world-wide best practice in how to use consultation not as a tool to 'manage' public opinion but as a tool for using public opinion to inform and influence decisions before they are decided. When done well, consultation enables people to express what they want from a decision, to shape the way the decision is made, to provide ways to match a decision to the consent of those affected and to stimulate new ideas and thinking from outside the 'usual suspects'. We need to break the link between those who make decisions and those who carry out consultation; it is only human nature that people who are making decisions will want to steer consultations towards what they believe is 'the right answer'. Instead an independent agency with the sole purpose of carrying out the best, most inclusive consultation possible should be set up entirely independently of the decision-makers (the Danish Board of Technology operate in this way). When decision-making processes begin consultation experts should advise on how and when the most effective consultation processes can be run. They can then be run to the highest standards possible and presented with the maximum transparency and clarity – even if the outcomes are not what decision-makers thought or hoped they would be.

Third, the way we prioritise what we spend our public wealth on is particularly important in shaping our society. Participatory budgeting is a way of ordinary people deciding what their priorities for investing public wealth are. For example, a local community could have open meetings (if it is over a certain size delegates could be elected from open meetings) to discuss and decide how to spend its local public investment budget; should they build a new swimming pool, or build more social housing? Participatory budgeting has had very positive impacts in the places where it has been implemented, especially in the city of Porto Alegre in Brazil where it has been successful in redistributing wealth and resource allocation from the richest to the poorest.

Fourth, it is not experts that should be in charge of informing public policy decisions but 'mini-publics'. A mini-public is a group that is made up of a cross-section of the population as a whole and reflects all of society to deliberate and come up with answers/recommendations on specific areas of public policy. There are different forms of mini-public but all use a process of providing evidence, views, advice, ideas and support so that ordinary members of the public can work towards an informed, balanced decision that has been thoroughly deliberated over. We use this system every day in Scotland to decide guilt or innocence in criminal trials; why don't we use the same system to decide the best course of action for a government? Imagine if we had a system where a small number of 'experts' (all of whom are particularly wealthy, most of whom are male and almost all of whom are older) would decide in private whether someone was guilty or innocent? It would be an outrage. So why is that the system we use to decide whether public services should be privatised, laws changed or wars started?

The best-known form of mini-public is the 'citizen's jury' in which a panel of people selected at random from the public as a whole are posed a question, given time and support to listen to lots of views on it, be provided with expert analysis, be able to call their own choice of witnesses and then be allowed to produce any kind of conclusion they see fit. They are now widely used and are shown to produce effective results. They do not bind the hands of government – they are only advisory – but they are a great way to get a wider range of views into decision-making processes. Other forms of mini-public such as planning cells, consensus conferences, deliberative polls and citizen assemblies have variations on this model at different scales but work on the same principles.

Using these approaches would be a fundamental and radical change in our democracy away from government by an elite and towards government by the people. Each should be used whenever there is a 'trigger moment' – for example, when an appointment has to be made a democratic method should be identified, when a new piece of policy work is started consultation experts should advise from the earliest stage and when governments seek advice they should use mini-publics. At first not every one will be used on every occasion but if they aren't used there should be a clear statement of why not. Eventually, participative government should become the norm.

Human rights are central to democracy. In Me-First politics they have become seen either as a 'gift' that can be handed down from a ruling class to ordinary people or as an imposition from 'faceless bureaucrats' who want to 'tick boxes'. This is the opposite of how a Common Weal culture of human rights would work. Human rights are not a top-down allowance but the shared understanding of the basis of healthy relationships between citizens, within communities and between individuals and the state. Much of what has gone wrong with democracy stems from a breakdown of trust between state and individual and that lack of trust has infected our other relationships. The ability to protect our individual right to be different and diverse and for that difference and diversity to be reflected and supported by all our public institutions is the glue that holds together our social contract. When 'social cohesion' (feeling like a community) works it does not look like lots of identical people in a sleepy consensus but lots of very different people living together as critically engaged citizens.

So just like contract law helps us have confidence that when we buy and sell things we know what acceptable behaviour is, human rights help us understand what is acceptable behaviour in our many and varied relationships with each other and with institutions. It is about creating trust and respect, two qualities that are absolutely essential to living in a good society. Some people say that we 'know' what is good and bad behaviour so there is no need to write it down, but we know murder is wrong yet we still have laws. Likewise, some people say human rights are 'only' about minority groups in society – but then that's like saying murder laws are 'only' about victims.

Human rights should be at the heart of a written constitution. All human rights should be informed by a continued firm commitment to the strongest international human rights standards, the historic substance of the Scottish legal system, and in consultation with ordinary people, communities and marginalised groups most likely to face human rights abuses. A major priority in this process should be the legal recognition of economic, social and culture rights like the right to education, housing, health and an adequate standard of living. These should be seen as rights rather than just 'services', in the same way as civil and political rights like the right to protest and right to organise in a trade-union.

As part of this Scotland could pave the way on issues of personal privacy and freedom from surveillance; the paranoid spy-state is unhealthy and must be challenged. Scotland could follow the lead of countries like Brazil by moving to publicly auditable open source software as standard to secure the data of both citizens and businesses. We could even pioneer legal protections for our environment and heritage.

All societies should be judged on how they treat their most vulnerable. The cruelty and indignity with which refugees have been treated by UK immigration and asylum policy is not tolerable in a civilised society. An end to detention centres, dawn raids and all other forms of mistreatment of those seeking asylum must end immediately, and the same rights as all other citizens – the right to education, employment and accommodation – should be guaranteed as their asylum request is being assessed.

A participatory democracy needs participative citizens. We shall see later how important it is to make sure people have time to participate, that

Using these approaches would be a fundamental and radical change in our democracy away from government by an elite and towards government by the people.

they're not overworked. In turn, we must emphasise this role of 'citizen' in our education system. Of course education is an important economic tool and giving pupils the ability to become effective, productive workers is a key part of an education system. But so is giving them the ability to become effective, involved citizens participating in democracy.

Education must emphasise not only 'learning to do' and 'learning to know' but also 'learning to be' and 'learning to live together'. It must ensure that citizens understand the structures and processes of their democracy and their society, that they are exposed to politics and political ideas, that they are given the confidence to be an active part of their local and national community. We invest in our physical infrastructure and our social infrastructure so we must also invest in our democratic infrastructure and that begins by investing in citizens. No part of that investment is more important than investing in their democratic education. This also means children should have rights to shape and influence their childhood and their schooling.

A functioning democracy also requires a functioning media. The ability to participate in democracy requires citizens to have effective access to information about their community and their society. Traditionally this was provided by broadcast and print media. Broadcast media is the media that is most often cited as the primary trusted source of information for citizens; it is where they get their basic information. Scotland needs a first-rate broadcast media if it wishes to have a properly functioning democracy. Investment in news, current affairs and documentary should be placed at the heart of public service broadcasting and sustaining a community of broadcast journalists over the long term is equally important. Citizens should have the right to shape broadcasting. In the Netherlands, member-based broadcasting associations share facilities and broadcasting time, both at national and local level, reflecting their membership and the diverse mix of society.

People then read the national print media to get access to views, ideas, opinion and argument. While you sometimes hear people claim that national print journalism is 'dead' in the era of social media, this is a dangerous proposition. Much of what is on social media comes from traditional media sources and that is because there has to be investment in news gathering, fact checking, editorial quality assurance and so on. We need a functioning daily national news media – the alternative is alarming. But the business model for most of the newspapers in Scotland is failing as readerships drop and costs rise. We almost certainly need to make public investment into national media to ensure it is secure. However this must not be on the terms of the unbalanced corporate media structure we have currently. Any public investment must be on the basis of supporting a diverse, plural media which reflects many different kinds of opinion. The ability for people to have easy access to different ideas and different opinions is every bit as important to democracy as freedom of speech.

Often when people talk about print media they think of the national dailies. But the local and regional media is just as important at holding to account local democracy and for informing people about what is happening in their communities. There are five major employers in mainland Scotland publishing well over one hundred weekly titles, with smaller companies publishing The Shetland Times, The Orcadian and West Highland Free Press on the islands. The importance of local newspapers for local democracy cannot be overestimated and as digital journalism develops at pace there are great opportunities to expand the influence of the media across Scotland. Civic Scotland does engage through local media but there is a growing interest by publishers to expand that engagement through use of local websites, which are linked to local titles. Most of this publisher interest is purely commercial but the opportunities for local and national campaigns to promote their case is growing at pace.

The National Union of Journalists is campaigning for increased staffing in these media companies to deal with the expansion into online and have introduced a new Modern Apprenticeship in Digital Journalism to help maintain quality and quantity of professional journalists. There is another opportunity tied to this development as the explosion of online journalism in Scotland has taken many by surprise. Pilot schemes have taken place moving the training into schools within communities and producing stepping stones into the MA process will allow publishers of all sizes to hire local, highly trained staff or freelancers who are aware of the legal and ethical requirements associated with the job. It is essential for local democracy that the councils and courts are covered by trained journalists and the local papers and their web sites have a role to play in holding politicians and authorities to account and reporting on the political and cultural needs of their area.

When we look at Scotland's media future we must start taking social media and online journalism more seriously. Online journalists, blogs and web-based news services need help and support if they are to be able to report and reflect on Scottish society. One possibility would be for the journalistic content of the national broadcast media to be made available as it is produced as an 'open source' resource (a bit like a news agency) which would enable innovative approaches to news media. This could support a proliferation of small, independent news blogs which use a broadcasting service's content as their starting point but who can develop that further by seeking their own reaction quotes or giving it their own spin.

The success of democracy also relies on the success of its institutions – the civil service, public agencies, local authority bureaucracies and so on. If we want a participative Scotland then these institutions must open up in ways that enable them to be participative. One approach would be to separate the 'blue sky thinking' aspect of these institutions (where they come up with ideas and solutions) and the administrative function (where they turn ideas into functioning policies and then implement and administer them). At the moment these tend to be combined in one process and managed by the same people, usually a small group of professional policy administrators without much wider involvement. The skills and specialisms of people who implement public policy must not be underestimated – the administration of public policy requires very specific knowledge. But that does not mean that knowing what should be implemented in the first place requires very specific knowledge. For example, how to run a large national health service requires complex skills but why we want the NHS and what we want from it is a conversation that everyone can engage in.

The process of shaping the underlying question ('what do we want to achieve?'), exploring the range of approaches ('how can we achieve it?') and devising solutions ('what do we have to do?') should become part of an open, national debate. One approach would be to set up national 'academies'

A Common Weal Scotland must be built on the redistribution of power so that citizens share in the decisions that shape their lives.

attached to universities each of which would specialise in a policy theme (communities, towns, planning and housing or education, training, skills and citizenship). If public bodies want to develop new policy thinking they could set these academies detailed specifications of what they want to achieve and then ask them to do the initial thinking and produce proposals. That process should be as open and inclusive as possible with democratic governance and the ability for anyone to engage – as well as drawing on the best academic expertise from here and abroad. It would then be for government to decide whether it accepts the proposals, adapt and change them if it wants to and then task policy administrators to put them in place and make them work.

All public life and all public administration should be expected to carry out the function of government in language that ordinary people can understand. If an average citizen with a high school education is unable to understand the content and intention of a government policy, then it should be considered fundamentally undemocratic. Politics and governance has descended into a habit of using a jargon-loaded vocabulary which can be impenetrable for outsiders. Legislation is written in legalistic terms when plain language would have been as easy to produce. There is an inherent assumption that citizens will never read or really care about the process of government so why bother making it understandable – a self-fulfilling prophecy if ever there was on.

The highest-quality public communication of the work of government should be seen as fundamental to democracy. A public agency should be set up to monitor all of the material being produced by government and its agencies to advise on how it can be produced and presented in plain language. That agency should also enhance the publication of government policy by presenting it in different ways – video clips, audio descriptions, animated films, public meetings or whatever best helps people to have the chance to understand what is being done on their behalf.

Finally, we need the best possible systems for making sure that influences on the political process are open and transparent. Lobbying is an important part of the democratic process but there is no reason for it not to be fully disclosed. Anyone engaged in seeking to influence public policy should have no concerns about disclosing their aims, their expenditure and the basic methods they plan to use to influence policy. Then we are able to see whether some groups or others are exerting an unfair or disproportionate level of influence. This does not only mean meeting with politicians but meetings with officials, expenditure on media campaigns, expenditure on data production and so on. There is no justifiable case for 'secret influence'.

A Common Weal Scotland must be built on the redistribution of power so that citizens share in the decisions that shape their lives. Social and institutional structures must be designed to support and enhance citizen's abilities to do that shaping in an informed way. Bunker politics must end.

Chapter Three

OUR PUBLIC WEALTH

Between us we can create the shared wealth to invest in
our society, our economy and our people

Share more of our national wealth through wages.

Make public finances strong with a high-wage economy.

Always pay our way – no more deficit.

Get Scotland's rate of investment up to international standards.

Use innovative methods of investment.

Set up a National Investment Bank.

Common Weal is the hope of a better future – and that is also the definition of investment. Investment is to expend time, effort or resource in the hope that it will create benefit in the future. We have to tackle the anti-investment culture, which takes from us that better future.

Investment means many things. We invest in people when we dedicate time and resource to improve their skills, knowledge and understanding, create security for them so they can flourish, to improve their access to what makes them happy and fulfilled. We invest in the household when we ensure economic security for families, affordable secure housing, proper time for family life, high-quality environments and strong communities. We invest in the community when we improve the infrastructure (especially open space and places for play and recreation), improve transport links, create conditions for positive relationships, strengthen local economies. We invest in our villages, towns and cities when we keep them alive with thriving high streets, great facilities, good public spaces, diverse economies and great transport links. We invest in the economy when we support long-term improvements in skills, productivity, innovation and trade, when we build new productive economic infrastructure (especially technology and plant), when we support export activity and diversification. We invest in the nation when we build infrastructure, improve public services, increase democracy and support thriving arts, culture, sport and entertainment. We invest in our environment when we protect biodiversity, open space, the fertility of the land, the management of our public space.

By no means is all of this investment public sector investment and it is not only about spending money. When you weed your garden you invest in the future of your environment. When you choose to do a night class you invest in your knowledge. When a business hires new, high-skill staff it invests in its productivity.

What investment is not is speculation. More often than not in Me-First economics vested interests refer to 'investment' when what they really mean is 'speculation'. Investment grows the totality – if you didn't do it, the total wouldn't be as big. It is a route to improvement. Speculation does not seek to grow the totality but simply capture a bigger share of it for yourself. So to 'invest in land' should mean 'to spend money making land better and more productive', not 'to buy land, do nothing with it and hope its value rises so it can be sold on to someone else unimproved'. Or to 'invest in a business' means to spend money on the business to improve it, not to buy it and strip it of its assets and sell it on.

This holds true when a corporation 'invests' not to create something that won't happen anyway but to make sure it happens in a way that benefits only the corporation. So to call multinational big business building and owning our energy infrastructure 'investment' is nonsense – the infrastructure must be built anyway and will be paid for by the same people (the consumers) so all big business is doing is reaping guaranteed profits from what is really public investment. If we let accountants, lawyers and big business redefine investment to justify predatory, socially and economically harmful behaviour then we will find ourselves stuck in a Me-First economics. They must be challenged relentlessly and asked where they are adding value, improving the totality. If they are not, then it is not investment.

Once we accept a real definition of investment our current track record on investment in Britain is shockingly bad. When you allow for 'depreciation' (the amount of money you would need to spend just to maintain things and keep them as they are) and an increasing population (which makes increasing demands on the infrastructure we have), Britain doesn't invest anything at all. This seems impossible but is true – the total spend of business, individuals and the public sector on investment is not currently enough even to maintain what we have in its current state.

In fact, for Scotland simply to reach the average rate of investment of a European nation we between us would need to invest at least £5 billion pounds more each year (private and public sectors combined). This means we have to boost both public and private investment rates. Below we will see how Scotland can kick-off a £100 billion investment programme.

First let us consider public investment.

Scotland's public wealth is substantial. It includes governmental budgets at both national and local levels and shared assets such as cooperatives, pension funds, mutuals, community enterprises, voluntary groups and more. All of this wealth is, in different ways, shared between people who have interests and goals in common. Most of it (though not all) is subject to some form of collective or democratic influence or control. One way or another, all of it is invested into making a better future.

Usually when we talk about public finance we only mean the budgets of national governments, so when we talk about public investment we assume that only refers to tax and spend. As we shall see, this is a silly way to look at public investment, but let's begin here.

Scotland's public finances, like those of the rest of the UK and much of the developed world, are widely considered to be under pressure – talk of 'the deficit' and 'budgetary constraints' is everywhere in our news coverage. Too often the heart of the problem is misunderstood to be an issue of public-sector overspend, when if we want to understand what is going on we should be really looking at why less and less comes in from tax.

The UK is a particularly unequal country – by some measures it is the fourth most unequal in the developed world. And we're the second lowest pay economy of the advanced economies. To put that in perspective, only one in five people working in Scotland today earn between £25,000 and £35,000 a year. Three out of five working Scots earn less than £25,000 a year and half earn less than £21,000. One in three working Scots earn less than £14,000 a year. If you earn £43,000 you are doing better (mainly much better) than nine out of ten working Scots. We have a chronic low-pay, unequal economy.

Meanwhile, if you lined up 100 people to represent the spread of wages in the Scottish economy and you started working upwards from the lowest paid you'd need to get to the 85th person before you'd come across someone who has less than 10 per cent of their income made up in some kind of benefit or tax credit.

In terms of tax, this is incredibly inefficient. As we shall see later, the annual cost of using tax credits to subsidise people earning the minimum wage of £6.31 an hour up to the living wage of £7.65 an hour is quarter of a billion pounds alone. We spend an incredible amount of national wealth subsidising low-pay employment. Meanwhile, because so few people are in well-paid employment, only a minority of people in work pay more in tax than they receive in tax credits, benefits and services. Low-pay economies put enormous pressure on public finances.

What would it look like if it was different? If you build a computer model of Scotland's income tax you can change different elements of it to see what would happen. If you keep the overall economy the same size (you don't grow the economy at all) but you distribute wages more evenly and have low unemployment (like in the Nordic countries) the impact on tax take is significant. In fact, if we had the pay and equality of the best of our neighbouring countries it would raise £4 billion more in tax without changing tax rates at all, even without growing the economy. That does not include the billions of pounds we wouldn't need to spend on benefits and tax credits – we'd have at least £5 or £6 billion pounds more to spend, enough to close the public finance deficit and improve public services. Me-First types always ask 'where does the money come from?'. This is where the money comes from.

Of course, it will take time to change the economy. During the transitionary period we need to find other ways to close the gap. As we have seen, because of the problems of low pay it would be difficult to raise that extra money by raising basic income tax (too few people can afford to pay more tax). But there are other taxes that can be used. It would be possible to raise about a billion pounds from Scotland's wealthiest citizens (and those who keep wealth and assets here) through a combination of a 50p higher tax rate, a 60p tax rate for those earning over £150,000 a year and a wealth or property tax. Much of this would be raised by taxing assets that were purchased with income that was untaxed at the time due to tax avoidance practices.

Up to a further billion pounds could be raised through various resource taxes: a Land Value Tax; a tax on profitable companies that use lots of natural resource like water; a tax on companies that benefit from planning decisions such as out-of-town supermarkets. There is a strong case for a special tax on the Scotch whisky industry which is incredibly profitable as a result of its purchase of Scottish heritage (85 per cent now owned by foreign multinationals) which could easily raise another £1 billion a year. A general rise in corporation tax is not proposed here – the contribution that business should make to stronger public wealth is by paying better wages and contributing more to employee pensions. All of these taxes would be targeted at those able to make that bigger contribution.

Investment grows the totality – if you didn't do it, the total wouldn't be as big. It is a route to improvement. Speculation does not seek to grow the totality but simply capture a bigger share of it for yourself.

There are three other sources of additional income to support public finances that could be found now. The first is to crack down on tax evasion and avoidance. This is easy to do. Much less generous definitions of who is 'resident' in Scotland would close down tax avoidance so that anyone who spends more than 183 days in the country would be eligible for full tax liability irrespective of whether they are a citizen or not. Multinational corporations, which can shift money across borders through internal accounting practices with the aim of avoiding tax, can be taxed on a proportion of their global turnover related to the size of their commercial activity in Scotland. So if a company makes five per cent of their sales in Scotland, we can tax them on the basis of five per cent of their global turnover, making tax avoidance impossible. We can permit tax collectors to ignore any accounting practice which is added with the sole purpose of reducing tax liability. And above all we can greatly simplify our tax system. The UK tax system is universally regarded as 'absurd' and has become so because the tax avoidance industry has had a scandalously powerful role in writing UK tax policy.

The second immediate source of income for Scotland is if we stop allowing private companies (usually foreign-owned) to capture all the value of our natural resources. It is crazy that we allow almost all the profits of our wind and tidal energy resources to flow straight into multinationals that immediately extract it from the Scottish economy. This is public philanthropy towards the super-rich on a breathtaking scale. If Scotland developed its renewable energy like a normal country – developing the big projects in collective ownership so all the profits flow back to the public – it would create a rapid new source of income.

The third is simply the process of re-prioritising budgets. The UK spends an exceptionally high amount of money on bad policy decisions – for example, renewing the Trident nuclear weapons system, a defence spend which is out of proportion or paying for the high financing costs and cor-porate profits of PFI deals. People often highlight the costs of moving from a Me-First politics (which doesn't invest) to an All-Of-Us-First politics (which sees investment as crucial) but fail to highlight the savings. Renegotiating PFI deals or taking them into collective ownership where finance is cheaper and there are no corporate profits or transferring unnecessary defence spending towards childcare instead will help improve public finances.

While it is difficult to assess the scale of income from renewable gen-eration, a tax avoidance crack-down or renegotiating PFI contracts, it is not unreasonable to expect it – along with the other taxes proposed above – to create enough income to not have to worry about public sector deficits and free up new revenue for investment.

So we must raise taxes on those best able to contribute to plug the gap immediately and then move rapidly towards a high-pay economy to get rid of the gap structurally and altogether. But that is not enough. Raising and spending public wealth has many very important roles. Of course it creates popular public services and national infrastructure and of course that stimu-lates the wider economy. But using public wealth to create national investment is incredibly efficient at creating jobs. As one senior CEO recently explained, the private sector will do almost anything else to increase profits before it will increase the number of jobs it creates. Indeed, in recent decades cutting jobs and spending more on advertising, marketing, restructuring or speculation has been one of the main drivers of corporate profits. So the United States spends twice as much of its national wealth on healthcare than we do in Britain but that expenditure creates fewer jobs proportionately than we do with half the spend. That is because the private sector will set prices not at what things cost but at the highest level they can. It is great at producing profits but very bad at producing jobs.

And it's not just that the public sector is good at creating jobs but that it is particularly good at creating high pay jobs. That is because many of the jobs created in public services are professional jobs (e.g. teaching, medicine, social work) and where they are routine jobs they still pay a better wage (in part because the public sector still has strong trade unions). And those jobs have a very important feature; because they do not depend on a 'market', they do not disappear during short-term economics dips. So when Britain went into recession the private sector shed a lot of jobs – but the public sector maintained jobs. This has what is known as a 'counter-cyclical effect' because it stabilises the amount of demand in an economy at precisely the time the private sector is removing demand.

Remember, it is not big-business profits that create wealth, it's work. And since the public sector is much more efficient at creating work, that means it is more efficient at creating wealth. We can see this in practice because all of our neighbouring countries with the most impressive economic performance spend a much higher proportion of their national wealth on public services than we do. And of course, greater investment in public services and public infrastructure create a lower cost of living (because together we act like a powerful buying consortium and save money) and a better society.

So as soon as we succeed in creating a high-pay economy we need to dedicate a proportion of that extra personal wealth to increasing public wealth through higher taxes. People will still be better off and will benefit from improved economic performance and better services and facilities. All the evidence shows that this package – better wages with higher taxes for better services – would be very popular.

This is how we create healthy public finances to support revenue spending. But that is only the beginning of how we start to invest in our society.

The politics of austerity has tried to confuse us all about debt, deficit, borrowing and investment. It has deliberately mixed up the difference between revenue and capital. Revenue is what you have to spend over and over again like paying wages, buying goods and services, maintaining infrastructure and paying finance costs. Capital is what you have to spend only once like building roads and bridges or new energy generation. Austerity politics has used comparisons with how we run a household to argue against investment, claiming you can't keep running up a credit card bill forever. Which is silly – you wouldn't buy a house on a credit card and you wouldn't buy your groceries with a mortgage. Austerity refuses to accept that there are different kinds of spending as a way to trick people into believing we can't spend.

Another trick of austerity politics is to confuse debt and deficit. Debt is to borrow money – like taking out a mortgage to buy a house. Deficit is when your expenditure is higher than your income – like if you couldn't afford to pay your mortgage payments any more. Deficit is bad – you should always try and stay within your budgets. Borrowing money to cover your deficit is very bad – you can't keep spending more than you have and covering it up with borrowing that gets higher and higher. Deficit-fuelled debt is borrowing to keep taxes low on the rich and to allow big corporations to keep dodging their tax responsibilities. A Common Weal Scotland should raise the taxes it needs to pay its bills and should not get caught in a cycle of deficit and borrowing.

However, just because deficit-fuelled debt is bad does not mean all debt is bad. A mortgage is debt, and yet it has improved many people's lives and made many people wealthier. Every big company in the world borrows money because it is the most effective way to invest. When you borrow to invest (and you do it right) the whole point is that you invest to create more wealth than the cost of the borrowing. In developed economies, borrowing is one of the main ways to create wealth. What is true in the private sector is also true in the public sector.

We can see this very clearly if we look at history. The periods where Britain had its best economic performance (the industrial revolution, the height of Britain's trading empire, the post-war boom) are the periods of by far the highest public borrowing. During these periods public borrowing was up to ten times higher than our public borrowing is now. Actually, we're living through one of the periods with the lowest public sector debt in Britain's history. But because in the past borrowing was used, not to pay for the costs of failing to raise enough money to pay the bills, but rather to invest to create wealth, these are also – by far – the periods when Britain was paying its debt off quickest.

Me-First politics hates public investment because public investment makes everyone better off. It favours a low-investment society where big commercial interests make wealth not from investment but from exploitation. It is get-rich-quick politics, the idea that doing nothing is a magic short-cut to creating wealth. It claims if we cut public investment somehow this will stimulate private growth. It sounds too good to be true – because it isn't true.

So how does a Common Weal Scotland invest? There are four ways we suggest this should be done.

Firstly, we need to ensure healthy revenue spending, which invests properly in public services but does not cause deficit-fuelled borrowing. How this can be done has been explored above. The first stage must be to ensure sound public finance to end the cycle of deficit budgets.

Then we need to identify three kinds of public investment. The first is investment for induced growth. Induced growth is where you invest in a way that does not create direct financial returns but will cause growth, which will increase tax take and so pay for itself. A good example of investing to create induced growth is childcare; free childcare doesn't generate profit but by creating lots of jobs as child-carers (especially because these would be comparatively well paid jobs) and by enabling more women to participate in the economy the investment will increase economic growth enough to cover the cost of the policy. Other labour market interventions (investment in workers and the workforce to increase growth) can achieve the same thing.

To invest in induced growth government should borrow. The costs of that borrowing should be met from revenue expenditure, eventually all being repaid by the growth induced in the wider economy. However, claiming willy-nilly that expenditure was creating growth that it didn't actually create is one of the reasons the UK has failed to managed its budgets. Induced growth investment must be carefully monitored to show that it creates the growth it aims to create. If growth falls short, the funding gap must be considered a subsidy and that subsidy must be added to revenue expenditure. This is simply a matter of good discipline.

The second kind of public investment is income-generating investment. There are all kinds of public expenditure that create direct income. For example, when you build public rented housing it generates rents. When you build electricity generation it is paid for by consumers. Investing to create new revenue streams which pay for the borrowing needed (and more) is essential to a national investment strategy.

To ensure discipline it would be possible to create self-contained national companies to borrow, invest in and manage these projects. A national housing company could borrow over 30 or 50 years, build high-quality housing and pay off the borrowing from rents. A national energy generation company (and lots of local companies) can borrow over 20 years against the value of the electricity generated. This creates immediate and on-going jobs, growth and income, which will be worth much more over time than the investment made. At any point government can also choose to subsidise this kind of investment – for example if it wanted to lower rents or the price of electricity. That would come from revenue expenditure.

So raise some taxes to get out of deficit and to invest in public services, borrow to invest in activity that stimulates growth that will pay for the borrowing, borrow to invest in projects that create enough income to cover the borrowing and start special publicly- and collectively-owned companies to set up special projects.

Finally, there are 'special projects' which Scotland might wish to invest in collectively which do not fall under the normal responsibilities of government. An example of this might be a collective decision we to try and stimulate a large-scale industry sector that the private sector is not growing fast enough. If Scotland decided that hydrogen-powered ships or a large-scale biomass industry or a containerised shipping business offer a real opportunity for Scotland's future we can create what are called 'Special Purpose Vehicles' to invest in these. An SPV is a kind of accounting structure which enables public money to be invested but the risk to be contained so that if anything goes wrong it is not the public purse that picks up the pieces.

An example of this might be a national mutual or local mutual company. This could be a company set up with investment from the public sector but would then be run like any other business, borrowing to invest on the basis of future profit. Every Scottish citizen (or community member in a local mutual company) could be given one non-tradeable share in that national company and would have a democratic right to vote on how it is run – and would get dividends from the profits of that company. It would be a limited company and not owned by the government so neither citizens nor the government would be liable.

So raise some taxes to get out of deficit and to invest in public services, borrow to invest in activity that stimulates growth that will pay for the borrowing (but make sure it really does create the growth), borrow to invest in projects that create enough income to cover the borrowing and start special publicly- and collectively-owned companies to set up special projects. This approach means we can both make a step-change in our rates of public investment and be prudent and sensible in managing our public finances at the same time.

This package enables us to up our public investment rates. Later on we will look at how to improve personal investment rates such as doing more training or learning new skills. But we also need to stimulate Scotland's poor record of private sector investment.

The financial services and banking sector has built its business case on the principle of fast returns on investment. It is not uncommon now to see investment time-scales in hours (when trading in financial instruments) when proper national investment needs to see investment time-scales in years or decades. Few banks now want to create ten-year lending relationships with customers – but these are the kinds of relationships that grow the kind of productive, manufacturing businesses Scotland needs to develop. If we don't have sources of patient, long-term finance then we need to set up a National Investment Bank (NIB).

A NIB has various advantages for investment over private banks. First, because it is Government-led its criteria for investment decisions are based on social goals rather than the interest of shareholders. For NIBs in neighbouring countries investment criteria have included the creation of employment, the promotion of technological innovation and the improvement of the environment. More detailed criteria could be added like the creation of high-wage jobs, industrial democracy and long-term commitments to the local economy. Private investors who are looking for funding from the NIB will have to prove they are helping towards these societal goals to get investment.

Second, a NIB would work with and support a network of local publicly-owned banks and savings banks (see more below) which would help identify and implement infrastructure investment priorities in their areas. That would mean investment in small businesses, co-operatives and mutuals which would otherwise not be able to get the required start-up funds. These businesses do not have high-profit returns like corporations, but they are job creators and stimulate local economies.

Third, NIB funding is cheaper and more stable than private banks because they source funds in the same way governments do: by issuing bonds. These bonds are guaranteed by the governments that own the banks and as a result are considered as safe as government bonds themselves. Not only does this allow the banks to provide inexpensive loans but it also ensures a stable supply of long-term financing for infrastructure projects.

Finally, NIBs have proven to be highly profitable, but because they are publicly owned the profit goes back to the government in the form of a dividend. That money can be put towards revenue expenditure to improve public services or it can go into capital expenditure to build major public infrastructure projects.

A NIB in Scotland would be capitalised by building upon the foundations – and assets – of existing bodies owned or jointly owned by the Scottish Government, such as the Scottish Investment Bank, the Green Investment Bank, the Scottish Futures Trust and the Royal Bank of Scotland (RBS). These could be converted into one unified investment bank. In addition to existing assets, the Scottish Government could issue bonds to capitalise the bank. Like other banks, the NIB would be able to lend multiples of its core capital. However, as many of its loans would be to public bodies for housing, energy and other projects which were exceptionally low risk and government backed, a higher lending multiple for the NIB of say 20 times core assets would be permissible, compared to commercial banks which being based on riskier investment should be restricted to 10 times assets. Thus if the NIB was capitalised at £5 Billion it could lend £100 Billion over 20 years without further capitalisation. NIB lending would not count against public debt.

To understand the potential of a NIB as a source of funding for investment we can look at the Kreditanstalt für Wiederaufbau (KfW), 80 per cent owned by the Federal Republic of Germany and 20 per cent owned by the Länder (German federal states). The bank raises around 60 to 70 billion Euros each year by issuing bonds, which makes it the fifth-largest capital markets issuer in Europe after the governments of the four biggest European economies. This is between 2.2 per cent and 2.6 per cent of German GDP. If a national investment bank in Scotland sourced funds of between 2.2 per cent and 2.6 per cent of its GDP this would provide a Scottish bank with a sum of between £3.2 and £3.7 billion per year. This would be a very serious level of investment in industry and infrastructure in Scotland, which would quite quickly begin to transform the nation.

A Common Weal Scotland must be built on the spirit of investment: of expending time, effort and resource now because we believe the future can be better than the present. We must use our public wealth to make that investment happen.

Chapter Four

AN INDUSTRIAL POLICY

How we can build a better economy that serves us all

38

Create a high-wage, productive, innovative economy with
industrial democracy by using an industrial policy.

Let sector forums lead policy development for industry.

Use an industrial policy toolkit to favour the kind
of economy we want.

Give much more emphasis to the importance of local
trade and local businesses.

Invest in manufacturing and 'smart specialisation'.

Promote a much more diverse ownership models for business.

Stop the 'brain drain' by investing in research and
development and our world class universities.

Anchor promising new industries in the Scottish economy.

The economy is a system for 'social provisioning', the process of taking
resources (raw materials and skills), turning them into the things that people
need and distributing them to the people that need them. When the economy is creating the things that people need and is getting them to the people
that need them, the economy is working. When people cannot get the things
they need the economy isn't working.

This fundamental explanation of how to recognise a successful economy has been lost among the lurid fantasies of Me-First economics. Me-First
economics is a system of 'social extraction', the process of taking out of society
as much wealth as possible in the shortest time possible with the least investment possible. That extraction process is called 'profit maximisation' – making
sure that you keep on taking more out than you put in. This wealth extraction
is falsely re-branded 'wealth creation' – we're told that if multinational corporations don't make ever-bigger profits the sky will fall in and we're led to
believe that the only measure of success is 'economic growth'.

In the strange world of Me-First economics everyone is supposed to
benefit from 'wealth extraction' because in the process of taking the wealth

out of the economy some of it is supposed to 'trickle down' to all of us who are not major shareholders in multinational corporations. That 'trickling' is supposed to take the form of jobs being created, taxes paid and goods and services bought. Unfortunately, the biggest wealth-extracting companies who tend to buy many of their goods and services from China have become very good at not paying tax and will do almost anything not to have to create more jobs if they can avoid it. Multinational corporations have become very good at not 'trickling' the wealth they collect from Scottish customers as they move it out of the country to their corporate headquarters 'offshore'.

The obsession with Me-First economics has had another damaging effect. Because it favours the maximum possible profit in the shortest possible time with the minimum possible investment, it is consistently advantageous for a certain kind of company. The kinds of company that benefit from Me-First economics are those that pay the lowest wages and require the least possible plant and technology (high skills and machinery require investment), that do not have a long-term strategy or purpose (short-term targets are always the priority), that are routine and low-risk (innovation takes time and effort), and that are big enough to bully smaller companies out of business (monopoly is great for profit). Me-First policies create a low-pay, low-productivity, low-innovation, low-investment economy with concentrated ownership.

This analogy of 'trickling down' is entirely the wrong one. The economy is much more like an active, organic system than a passive one which involves random 'spills' of wealth trickling down a static structure. The heart pumps blood round the body, it doesn't 'trickle-down' from top to bottom. To sort out our economy we need to get its heart working again.

As we have seen, high-pay jobs are what a Common Weal Scotland is built on. High-pay is built on four major factors. Firstly, it is productive jobs that are high-quality jobs. Productivity is a measure of how much added value is created by an employee per hour of work. Taking consumer goods out of a warehouse and stacking them up on a shelf only adds the value of how much the price is marked up. Because none of the value is added by the skill of the worker, you aim to pay the worker as little as possible. Whereas, if you are programming a computer game you create value out of almost nothing purely through your skills. Because it is your skill that creates the value you tend to be well paid.

Productivity is about doing things better, either because we improve how we work or we do new, more effective, work. Rebalancing the economy away from low-skill sectors like retail and low-productivity sectors like property speculation towards high-skill sectors like computing or high-productivity sectors like manufacturing creates better paid, more rewarding work.

Secondly, a high-pay economy has a high level of innovation. Innovation is about finding new ways to do old things or finding ways to do new things. There are three reasons why innovation creates a high-wage economy. Firstly, innovation improves productivity. Sometimes that is because of complex new processes or clever new products but often it is just about being open to change from old habits. So a new computer system might improve deliveries and increase sales, but so might simply looking to see if you can do your deliveries in a different order enabling more deliveries each day.

The second reason innovation helps create higher wages is that innovation is driven by people – it is a skill and innovative people add more value so tend to earn higher wages. Some of that is scientists in laboratories and some of it is people who can operate complicated computer systems. But in really effective economies the vast majority of innovation is employee-driven innovation and the vast majority of it is comparatively routine – if we move this here we can fit more in, if we do it in this order we can save more time, if we build it like this it'll save money. An economy that treats all workers as a source of innovation and rewards them accordingly is more successful.

And of course the third reason innovation is so important is that it is where the future economy is born. Innovation today creates products and processes which create jobs tomorrow – and the right kinds of jobs.

The third factor in creating a high-pay economy is investment. As we have seen earlier, investment is key to creating a better economy. Short-termism and investment-aversion condemn economies to stagnate, discourage the most promising industry sectors and skews the economy towards a low-pay spiral.

Finally, ownership is important. Me-First economics not only expresses no interest in how and where enterprises are owned but actively discourages discussion of ownership. In that world view 'the market has spoken' and whoever is left standing must be 'the right outcome'. It means that Scotland has an economy, dominated by big multinational corporations at

The heart pumps blood round the body, it doesn't 'trickle-down' from top to bottom. To sort out our economy we need to get its heart working again.

the top, lots of self-employed micro-businesses at the bottom and very little in between. When a Scottish company grows and becomes competitive, often it is bought by a bigger, foreign-owned company, which then strips its assets and exports its jobs. Meanwhile in retail, energy, food distribution, transport, banking and other sectors the market is controlled by such a small number of giant corporations that monopoly and cartel behaviour is common. This tends to export jobs and profits and leaves an unbalanced economy vulnerable to decisions made by a tiny number of enterprises.

Foreign-owned companies take profits out of the economy while domestically-owned companies tend to keep profits in the economy. Multinational companies are much more likely to have supply chains outside the economy, independent businesses are much more likely to rely on supply chains inside the economy. Public Limited Companies (PLCs) are much more likely to emphasise dividend to shareholders, mutual and cooperative companies are much more likely to emphasise investment for the long term. Diversity of ownership and size creates a much more effective and robust economy than a monolithic corporate economy.

As well as these factors that create high-pay jobs, there are factors that create stability and resilience. Me-First economics obsesses over 'global trade'; and yet local trade makes up a much larger proportion of the economy and sustains many more jobs. Of course we need both but the corporate capture of local trade has killed local economies.

On the international scale, If Scotland is to pay its way in the world it needs to export. The pretence that selling financial derivatives was the same as exporting must come to an end and we need to take our balance of trade seriously again. Whatever we do, it cannot be one thing but many things. Again and again we've seen that relying too much on a few industry sectors is too risky – if something happens to harm one industry the rest of the economy isn't strong enough to pick up the slack.

So this is our challenge: how to create a high-wage, high-productivity, high-innovation, high-investment economy based on diversity of ownership and enterprise type with many different industry sectors. Me-First economics claims this can't be done; that only the free market can shape the economy. This view sees the economy as beyond democracy, something wholly-owned by multinationals. It is wedded to the idea that government must be 'neutral' when it makes economic policy, not seeking to influence or change the market.

But there is no such thing as economic neutrality. Every decision made will favour one kind of activity or another. If public contracts are big, only big companies can win them; if public contracts are small, small companies have more chance. We just have to start making decisions that favour the kind of economy we want.

Me-First economics is also obsessed with 'magic button' solutions, one simple action which will fix everything, almost always at the top level. So 'deregulation' will solve everything – just because it will. Or low interests rates will solve everything – just because they will. Or cutting public expenditure will solve everything – just because it will. In reality, there are no magic solutions – to have an All-Of-Us-First economy we need to improve all areas of potential economic development. The 'Wizard of Oz' economic management of one man sitting behind a curtain, pulling levers which control everything is a damaging delusion.

So what is the alternative? You reject the idea that it is damaging to steer the economy. You recognise that every decision works towards one economic outcome or another. You let go of the belief that the economy can be managed entirely from the centre. You accept that it is the job of a democracy to provide a good jobs for everyone. You embrace the capacity of all sectors of the economy to improve. You stop believing that the only way to grow an economy is by letting the most powerful companies push everyone else aside. You focus on the reality that every sector of the economy is different and that every sector needs different approaches to success.

You create an industrial policy.

An industrial policy is a plan that looks at the full range of policy decisions and choices (not just economic policies but also things like housing, procurement, childcare, welfare, energy and so on) and develops a plan which uses those decisions and choices where appropriate to seek to favour a specific kind of economy.

An industrial policy is not a centrally-planned approach – if an industry sector needs different approaches in different geographical areas then an industrial policy should reflect that. Nor is it a centrally-managed approach – it is not delivered by a small team in one building tweaking the same small number of policies. It is not a top-down approach – it can only be built up by bringing together the key players in the industries themselves. It is not isolated – it must be wholly and fully integrated with other big policy strands that affect economic improvement like industrial democracy and welfare. But it is active – where intervention is required it will intervene.

All of this means that it is not for theorists or policy-wonks alone to create an industrial policy but that an industrial policy must be built up mutually and collectively by anyone who can help to improve the economy. This is therefore not an outline of an industrial policy but the outline of how we build and industrial policy and what we'd want it to achieve.

So how do we build an industrial policy? Through sector forums. A sector forum is a policy-designing body made up of all the key players in an industry sector. Those players may include multinational corporations, large independent businesses and small- and medium-sized independent businesses, employees, trade unions, universities, colleges and schools, training provider, supply chain companies, local authorities, community representation and consumer groups.

A sector forum covers only one sector of the economy – food production or biotechnology or tourism or shipbuilding. Each sector forum would be supported with expertise and resource from a national economic development agency but – crucially – it isn't the agency creating policy advice after consulting a forum but the forum making the decision directly with the support of the agency. Each forum would submit its sector plan to government directly – neither government agencies nor often unrepresentative business representative groups need act as intermediaries.

These plans help inform government but it is for government and the sector forums to discuss and negotiate changes directly. Sector forums begin by taking a mutual approach – all the stakeholders involved may have some competing interests and may even be in direct competition but it is possible to identify and focus on mutual interests and it is this that forums are seeking to make progress on. The aim is to create as effective an environment as possible for all to work within so it improves the success of all.

The aim is to create as effective an environment as possible for all to work within so it improves the success of all.

The sector focus is important; different industry sectors may face completely different challenges with low productivity and innovation being a brake on progress in one sector, need for investment in physical infrastructure being the biggest issue in a second or the need to diversify out of a declining market the priority for a third. We currently have an uneven economy in which some sectors are very advanced and have invested to modernise – and others are stagnant. To get all of the economy improving it is important to recognise that we have highly uneven economic development.

A final, important aspect of sector forums is precisely that they do not 'pick winners' by focussing only on glamorous, large or profitable industry sectors but recognise that really effective economies improve every sector of the economy, no matter how routine or boring they seem. Any part of the economy can become better if we look at the drivers of productivity, the role of innovation, the benefit of investment and the potential added-value of employees. When we can get economies to 'grow up together' like this, improving consistently across all aspects, you get a more resilient and integrated economy with better articulation across sectors. Which is just to say that if all businesses are advanced and improving they are much better able to work with each other.

Just because this does not provide the detailed content of an industrial policy does not mean that it is difficult to understand the kinds of tools that are used to construct that policy. An industrial policy toolkit is a list of the different policy tools that can be used – the following are only some examples.

Monetary Policy can be used to encourage finance to take a more long-term approach to the economy. It can be used to make exports more competitive, direct more bank investment towards the productive economy and to stabilise and regulate the volatile financial services sector.

Fiscal policy can be used to equalise the tax burden facing different businesses by ending tax evasion. It can be used to create targeted incentives or to put in place VAT reduction for industry sectors which run on low margins, such as tourism and hospitality.

Finance and investment are crucial. A national investment bank is central to an industrial strategy to provide patient, long-term finance to emerging and growing enterprises. As discussed above, there are a number of other models for creating investment vehicles such as special vehicles for collective national and community borrowing. A national investment bank can partner with a network of community banks in lending and sharing risk in financing promising local start-up businesses.

Natural resource management offers many opportunities in fishing, oil and gas, land, renewables, sea-bed, food, whisky and forestry. For example, a land value tax could be used to more closely align the cost of land and its economic value, making it economically viable for people to set up land-based enterprises.

It is important that we stop losing many of our promising new industry sectors through equity takeover, which exports the jobs and intellectual assets, so we need 'anchoring strategies' which keep new industries in Scotland. Competition policy can help reduce takeovers, as can the use of equity stakes in finance arrangements and employee involvement in company governance. Competition policy can also be used to ensure greater diversity in the economy.

There are different approaches to market development that can be used to help support emerging enterprises by securing order books for them. Public procurement is particularly important and should be used as a key economic development tool. But other strategies to encourage local sourcing can help with local trade while export support can help with international trade.

Economic development agencies can be used more effectively to pursue the desired economy. They can be set more structural goals such as specific aims to diversify the economy both by sector and enterprise type and size. They can be given a more mutual focus in supporting sector forums and take a particular focus on achieving smart specialisation.

We can make much better use of innovation, research and development and Scotland's world-class universities. Five Scottish universities are in the world's top 200, one-sixth of the UK's representation in the top 200. UK expenditure on research and development has been in steady decline, down to 1.7 per cent of GDP. That compares to 2.7 per cent in the US, 2.8

per cent in Germany and 3.4 per cent in Sweden. A one per cent increase in investment in research and development will allow Scotland to maximise the potential of its world-class universities and encourage graduates to stay and work in Scotland.

The sector forum approach is particularly helpful in creating the cluster strategies, which help the development of high-tech start-ups which spin out of universities and research and development investment. Take the IT Industry as an example, where we have five-star rated university courses producing 4,800 highly-skilled computer science graduates a year, but we only have 70,000 IT workers – just fifteen years' worth of graduates.

There are a wide range of ways of encouraging better use of innovation on the part of businesses by using tax incentives, conditions of licensing of public resources, ways of managing intellectual property law and programmes for encouraging the employment of innovation-focussed graduates. It also cannot be stressed enough that much of the most useful innovation which transforms enterprises comes from employee innovation, a capacity which is best unlocked through industrial democracy.

Regulation can be used to stabilise the finance sector, which is key to the economy but is currently risky and volatile. Regulation can also prevent monopolistic practices, encourage diversity, help improve innovation and productivity and encourage high-value economic activity.

A proper system of industrial democracy can improve productivity and innovation, anchor businesses through governance arrangements and improve the competitiveness of enterprises.

Education, training and skills strategies for business can be led directly by the relevant industry sector forums. We can focus on much more bespoke collaborations between sectors and individual enterprises and universities and colleges. A national shift to encourage pupils to study engineering, maths, computing and design would also increase human capacity. Active labour market policies of this sort would also include childcare to increase female economic participation. We should also be making much better use of 'build and train' contracts where service companies are contracted to carry out work which we do not currently have the indigenous capacity to do, but training up indigenous capacity for the future is part of the contract.

Proper social security can support a high-wage economy by eradicating the culture of fear and anxiety that lowers confidence and creates a

Every aspect of the economy will get the habit of seeking to improve all the time, improving the quality of service people experience continually. This will drive up both productivity and demand for quality.

'race to the bottom' in the labour market and create a culture of security which creates the foundation for people to seek and pursue better economic options. A citizen's Income will also boost enterprise development by offering people who seek to start businesses some financial security during the period when enterprises are establishing themselves.

A diversification strategy (including some specific diversification agencies in areas such as shipbuilding and defence manufacture) can help to change the balance of the economy. This can be both a whole-economy strategy and a whole-sector strategy but can also offer support for individual business diversification.

So if this is the range of tools which we can use to build, what might the economy we build look like? It is important to note that the following is just an illustration of what a Common Weal economy might seek to be like – but being able to envisage an economy different from the one we have is important.

A Common Weal economy would begin by getting local trade right. Local businesses will be much better at supplying each other and will take the lead in supplying public bodies with local produce with much more emphasis placed on the need to keep local business local. This will lead to an expansion of local food production with many more growers supplying local bakers, microbreweries, artisan food makers and so on, all selling to local consumers. Everything from garage services to trades and retail will be available locally, mostly locally owned.

Less emphasis will be placed on spending on imported consumer goods and more on spending on activity such as domestic tourism, entertainment, arts and culture, eating and drinking, hobbies and pastimes where the economic benefit remains in our economy.

Every aspect of the economy will get the habit of seeking to improve all the time, improving the quality of service people experience continually.

This will drive up both productivity and demand for quality. The default position will not be 'how can we improve profits by driving down costs and pay' but 'how can we improve business effectiveness by harnessing skills and doing things better' – for example, retailers trying to find out what skills their employees can add to the productivity of their business, perhaps by devolving more management to the shop floor.

There will be much more manufacturing at many different scales. Scotland needs to re-industrialise. We will seize national opportunities to build big new manufacturing industries but we will also see a proliferation of small, specialist manufacture such as micro-engineering and prototyping. We will also develop other value-adding industries (like computing and research and development) which may not turn into manufacturing industries.

We will compete internationally on the basis of 'smart specialisation', identifying where specialising into a high-skill area can make enterprises more competitive – for example, we may not be able to compete with the Koreans in manufacturing bulk orders of ferries but we can out-compete them if we specialise in developing specialist hydrogen-powered electric ships.

Diversity of ownership will be normal with much more of the economy represented by the higher-performing mutual and cooperative business models and with a much better balance of sizes. Economies will reflect their local environments with greater uses of community cooperative and social enterprises in areas where the local economy is weak.

Where there is monopoly or a tendency to monopoly there will be collective ownership or at least much greater collective control. Industries that rely on captive consumer demand like energy or transport will be structured so that the benefits are shared in the economy by all, not extracted from the economy by a few.

These collective industries will then be used to stimulate new industry sectors – for example, once we have collective ownership of energy we can create a manufacturing industry in Scotland to build and install the generating and storage infrastructure. And public expenditure will be used to stimulate other new sectors – for example, to set up German-style precision house-building factories to build public housing and retrofit old housing with new heating technologies.

The economy will be built not on the unfettered exploitation of consumers but on the careful and sustainable utilisation of our resources – natural, human and geo-strategic. Much of our collective wealth will be built on land, wind, tide, wave, water – and even more built on skill, innovation, creativity and design skills.

Finance will be patient and long-term, enabling businesses to take a longer-term approach to planning. Industrial democracy (including better company governance) and welfare reform will drive innovation and productivity. Promising developing industries will be 'anchored' into the economy and protected from buy-out.

We will not wait to take advantage of exciting new industry sectors like the manufacture of hydrogen fuel cells, the development of biomass farming, emerging space and robotics technologies, advanced material manufacture, shipping and specialist shipbuilding and so on. Where these and other industries are failing to develop we will act to stimulate them.

All of this is possible. A Common Weal Scotland can be built on a high-wage, high-productivity, high-skill, high-investment, diverse and sustainable economy. But the market alone has created an economy that tends in the opposite direction. To reverse these failures we must have an industrial policy.

Chapter Five

SHARED SCOTLAND

The things we rely on for a decent life should be
made to work for us

Make universalism the defining principle of public service.

Take energy back into collective ownership in a decentralised model.

Build new generation of heating technologies in collective ownership.

Start a large-scale programme of high-quality public sector rented housebuilding.

Make sure every household has access to a phone line and basic internet service.

Stimulate the transition to a hydrogen-powered, collective, high-quality transport system.

Put in place a food system that brings health, wellbeing and real economic benefit.

Reform land ownership to make land productive again.

There are some parts of the economy that are so essential to our individual and collective wellbeing that they cannot be left to markets alone. Electricity, heat, communications, transport, food, land and housing are not optional extras that people can take or leave but essential to survival.

There are also some parts of our society which are so important that they are now essential to modern life – education and healthcare, local and national infrastructure, policing and justice and so on. In modern times these have been treated as the foundation of national wellbeing and have been protected from markets that would exploit their importance to extract more profit.

These are the foundations of modern life – to be fed and warm and sheltered in somewhere decent to live, with electricity, a phone, a postal service and transport links, to be educated, to be cared for when we're ill, to have personal security, to live in a properly-equipped nation. These foundations can be used either to make us richer or poorer.

Unfortunately, they're being used to make us poorer. Because we have absolutely no option but to have access to these goods and services there is always a very high risk of monopoly provision being used to exploit citizens. The more these services have been left to the market, the greater the level of monopoly and cartel behaviour, the more exploited we have become. In almost all cases the market position of the biggest players (in energy, telecoms, post, transport, supermarkets, volume house build and more, fewer than six corporations dominate the market) have either pushed prices up for customers (in energy, housing and transport) or have closed down competition and exploited suppliers (the big supermarkets forcing farmers to sell at prices that lose them money). Telecoms and post are heading the same way. In all cases the profits made from the essential foundations of our lives are now taken away from us and given to corporations. Even the public services that were protected from market exploitation are no longer safe with an ever-increasing infiltration of the public sector by profit-extracting corporations.

This is not how it would be in a Common Weal Scotland. Rather than seeing the essential needs of citizens and asking 'how can their shared need make someone rich?' it would ask 'how can our shared need make us all richer?'. These foundations of our society are shared – we all pay for them all of the time, no exceptions – so the benefits should be shared. This 'shared Scotland' is the foundation for everything else. It provides the comfort and security that are the basis of a good life and the human and physical resources that underpin the economy.

The fundamental principle that binds shared Scotland together is 'universalism'. It is a simple principle – from the cradle to the grave, from each according to ability to pay to each according to need. So whoever you are, so long as you live in Scotland, from the day you are born to the day you die, you are backed up by great services paid for through public wealth. Your wealth is irrelevant – millionaire or poor pensioner – if you need healthcare you'll get healthcare, if you need education you'll get education, if you need to drive along a road the road will be maintained for you. It is a system that ties us all together in common interest, no matter who we are.

Fairness comes not from denying universal services to some people to 'punish' them for being better off but from paying for universal services through progressive tax that asks the better off to foot a larger proportion of the bill. It is a very simply principle that is under constant attack – universal services paid for with progressive taxes. It is fair and effective – the effectiveness comes from how the money is spent, the fairness from how it is raised. Excluding people from universal services does not make them 'fairer'; cutting tax most certainly does not make them more effective.

So why are universal public services so effective? The first reason is that they are incredibly efficient. Because everyone has a right to these services they are very cheap to administer – means-testing, refusing services, dealing with appeals and policing a selective system are all very expensive. The cost of mistakes and fraud is also much lower – if you compare the selective pension to the universal pension, error and fraud alone are more then 50 times higher. One of the reasons that selectivity (mean-testing people before they are allowed services) is so popular with some is that it is very expensive, with all the costs of doing means-tests going to corporations.

The second impact is that universal services have much better economic consequences. They are 'countercyclical' – which is to say that because they are always there they prop up the rest of the economy when there are economic difficulties. They are extremely efficient at creating good jobs. They make people more economically independent which is good for the economy. They have a very strong 'multiplier' effect (every pound spent on universal services creates a particularly high amount of economic activity elsewhere in the economy).

Universal public services also create good outcomes. 'Merit goods' are things which none of us creates alone but all of us benefit from collectively. For example, if we fall and break our leg then we benefit from the fact that universal public services educated doctors who can help us and educated enough of them that we know we'll be able to get access to one. 'Public goods' are things which just wouldn't happen if we didn't do them collectively. For example, if we hadn't pooled public wealth, who would have built and maintained our motorway system? These are both benefits we all receive from universal public services even if we didn't personally benefit from any single service. They create a better society and that benefits us all.

Universal public services are very important to improving equality. One of the most common arguments from people who want to end universal public services is that the money spent on 'middle class' service users is somehow being taken from 'the poor'. This is factually incorrect – the money being spent on all service users is being taken disproportionately from the

Universal public services are something we all share, that bring us together, that stop us blaming each other, that take away stigma and humiliation, that offer dignity for all. The act of saying 'no, you're not like the rest of us, you're poor, you need to join another queue' does the poor no favours whatsoever.

better off through progressive taxes. But also it simply doesn't match up with reality. There is a phenomenon known as 'the paradox of redistribution'. This shows over and over again that targeting resources at poorer groups makes them poorer while targeting them at everyone makes the poor disproportionately better off. The reason is very simple – if you give £100 pounds to everyone it makes by far the biggest difference to the poor, while if you give only the poor £100 other people quickly demand you stop doing it. The lesson is very simply; if everyone benefits, the poor benefit most and everyone supports it so it stays strong. If only the poor benefit it doesn't have support and soon they lose it. The poor do best when they are not made a special case. The same is true for gender equality; universal public services disproportionately benefit women and make them more economically independent.

Finally, universal public services are at the heart of a Common Weal Scotland because they are the very embodiment of what putting All-Of-Us-First looks like. It is by creating solidarity across society that we bring to an end the war of all against all that has divided us and weakened us. Universal public services are something we all share, that bring us together, that stop us blaming each other, that take away stigma and humiliation, that offer dignity for all. The act of saying 'no, you're not like the rest of us, you're poor, you need to join another queue' does the poor no favours whatsoever.

For all of us, from the cradle to the grave, given according to need, paid for according to ability; the world has achieved no more noble a sentiment for society.

We should state clearly what public values are sheltered under the umbrella of universalism – and we might even want to enshrine them in a constitution. Education and healthcare, policing and justice, the maintenance of our national infrastructure (especially roads and transport), childcare, social security income; these are the starting point for a national debate on the values of public service we believe to be fundamental to our nation.

Outside the realm of public services there is much we should protect from the full force of the market. Sometimes that means we should take collective ownership, sometimes it means we need better regulation and policy. In all it means we need much more collective control.

Electricity is an essential part of modern life, something we cannot live without. And yet the UK is the only nation in Europe that does not own its national grid – plus we pay the fourth highest electricity prices and have the lowest levels of satisfaction with the private companies that supply our electricity. The extent to which these companies have pushed prices higher and higher and have seen increasing corporate profits makes dissatisfaction inevitable.

The UK electricity system is a messy series of market subsidies, price regulation and crossed fingers. We privatised everything and then had to balance bribing electricity companies with a system of guaranteed profit to get them to invest in infrastructure and regulating prices so that consumers don't rebel. So we have a regulator that nominally stops electricity prices rising too fast but has an even greater role in making sure that consumer prices guarantee companies a healthy profit. The regulation lets them pass on all their costs (and more) to the customer and add on guaranteed profit. The consumer can do nothing at all about it. This is risk-free monopoly capitalism; a company almost literally can't lose. Meanwhile we're not even free to plan our own energy system – we just have to hope we've bribed the private companies enough to create the infrastructure we need. And if we haven't we need to come up with a bigger bribe.

This makes no sense at all, either in terms of knowing we'll have future, secure energy supplies or in trying to create a just society. Thankfully, there is an easy solution.

There are three models for electricity supply outlined by the EU – all nationalised, a nationalised grid with contracts for services companies to maintain or fully privatised (the EU warns against this last option). The UK is the only all-privatised system. It would therefore not only be within EU rules to take the grid into collective ownership, the EU encourages it. It would cost only a fair rate of compensation – and since the companies have already passed on most of their costs to consumers any additional compensation would be low.

What is not proposed is the nationalisation of the energy companies that service the grid (Scottish Power and Scottish and Southern Energy) since this would be much more expensive. Rather they should be given simple fixed-price contracts to maintain the grid. We would collectively decide what we want from our energy sector and pay them to build and maintain it. The planning for our electricity needs would be done by a Scottish Energy Agency. A public sector Scottish Energy Generating Corporation would own the grid and would develop the new large-scale generating capacity needed. It would contract companies to maintain the grid and sell electricity to the consumer at a set price.

Taking electricity generation back into collective ownership over time is easy since virtually all the energy generation capacity we currently have will need to be replaced over the next 20 years. Since we'll have to pay for all this new generation capacity one way or the other (all costs are passed on to the consumer), the real question is whether we want to own it collectively and keep the profit collectively or let private companies keep the profit instead. Why we'd consider letting the private companies keep it is difficult to understand.

Creating generation infrastructure gives us an opportunity to fix the mistakes of the past. Large, centralised, monolithic organisations have been shown to be vulnerable, slow to innovate, inefficient and poor at reflecting diversity of need. This is especially true in energy where we have always been overly-reliant on a small number of large generating facilities. Small-scale renewable generation along with energy storage technologies mean we can now move towards a 'de-centred' grid system. Local communities can have their own generation capacity through local energy companies owned either by local authorities or cooperatively at community level. They can integrate energy storage technologies and so can become partially or wholly energy self-sufficient. It would give both local and democratic control of energy systems. Large-scale and off-shore generation will still be owned and managed at a national level.

This diverse, de-centred energy system is much more resilient and efficient. It is also much cheaper – because it would be developed by the public and kept in public ownership the finance costs alone would be 20 per cent cheaper, and of course all the profits come back to the public. Compared to the complex corporate-friendly UK energy market, Scottish electricity would be generated and distributed much more cheaply.

Energy storage is also an important emerging link in Scotland's energy security. Particularly because of Scotland's enormous resources in renewable energy, generation is only half the question. Widespread, localised energy storage infrastructure would greatly increase the efficiency of renewable generation (you don't have to dump electricity generated at the 'wrong time'). This would mean both better value for money for the generation we put in place and big savings by not having to build as much generation capacity as we otherwise would need to. Technologies like Liquid Air Storage are also extremely responsive and can be used to turn electricity supply up or down almost instantly.

Finally, cheaper, cleaner, more reliable electricity which we control and the profits of which come back to us is only the beginning of the potential benefits of owning our own electricity system. Because we currently have no control we can't use the electricity system as an economic development tool. At the moment foreign companies buy foreign technology, put them on land owned by rich people and then take all the profits from consumers. If we owned the grid we could choose to build all the technologies here (we would easily be able to use R&D opt-outs from EU rules given the importance of renewable energy to Scotland's economy). A major programme of energy storage would pay for itself and would create at least 5,000 high-quality jobs immediately. Many more again could be generated if we were building other renewable technologies here.

As we all know, Scotland has not seen the benefit from the oil discovered in its territory. Quite why we are allowing 'inward investment' to repeat the same mistake over again for our renewable industry is a mystery.

The model for non-electricity-based energy supply would be similar but even more localised. Again, with gas and oil supplies proving volatile and vulnerable and with the need to reduce our carbon emissions, investment in a major new era of heating technologies is essential and will happen anyway. Again the question is not if but how we make that investment. The same principles apply – public borrowing is much cheaper than private borrowing so public investment is much cheaper than private investment. We should plan collectively rather than hoping private companies get it right on their own.

The system should not be designed to take the maximum amount of money away from customers. If there is to be benefit coming from something we all need then we should all share that benefit collectively.

Where heating is more complex is in the range of technologies and associated practices involved. Electricity is electricity but we can heat using a range of different sources, different delivery mechanisms – and it is affected by a wider range of associated actions. Plus all of this is heavily influenced by geography. Where there is higher density housing (especially blocks of flats and tenements), district heating is particularly effective. District heating works by creating one big heating source for each block of flats or street and then delivering hot water to each via insulated networks of pipes. One large-scale heating source is much more efficient than many small heating sources and it enables better technologies to be used.

The heating source itself can vary and groups of heating sources be used at once. Among the options are biomass (particularly where space is available), solar thermal, geothermal (particularly where there are old mineshafts), hydrogen gas, excess electricity and so on. And heating is very greatly affected by issues such as house design and insulation, which means heating policy must be closely tied to housing and planning policy.

Housing is a particular problem for Scotland. House prices here have been driven ever upwards by the use of housing as a means of speculation. Over the course of the last 40 years public policy has primarily treated housing as an issue of trade and profit; the role of the house as somewhere to live does not seem to be reflected in policy. So if you are a developer and you want to knock down a house and build a new one you don't pay any VAT. But if you live in a house and you want to improve it, you pay full VAT. Success in housing is measured almost entirely by how successful the trade in housing has been – house prices rises, increases in sales, number of new units on the market.

This has two major impacts. The first is that it has created a major transfer of wealth from the many to the few. If you own one home then rising house prices doesn't really help you – your house may be worth more on paper but if you sell it the price of finding somewhere else to live has risen in exactly the same way. Only your mortgage provider is sure to make a substantial profit. It is the property developer or property speculator who has made the real profit. By buying up land and controlling the supply of housing,

Cheaper, cleaner, more reliable electricity which we control and the profits of which come back to us is only the beginning of the potential benefits of owning our own electricity system.

developers have been able to capture all of the social value that housing creates. Higher house prices have only increased greatly the amount of social value that has been extracted by developers. The same is true of buy-to-let or property speculation (the buying and selling of houses for profit). In all these industries large commercial players have been able to manipulate the housing market to increase their profits by controlling the supply of an essential need of life – somewhere to live. And remember, all of these profits have been derived from the pockets of home-owners – the rising price of your house is making you poorer, not richer.

Thirty years ago, for every £100 of public money spent on housing, £80 went on bricks and mortar and £20 went on housing benefit. So most of the money was spent increasing the supply of housing to enable people to get access to affordable homes and a minority of money was given as emergency support where affordable homes were not available. Now, for every £100 of public money spent on housing, £95 goes on housing benefit and £5 goes on bricks and mortar. So most of the money goes straight to property owners who control housing supply and virtually none goes to expanding the supply of housing. This pushes up rents and house prices, the opposite of what public policy should be seeking to do.

The outcome of all of this is that the UK now has some of the world's highest housing costs, and virtually all of the benefit of these costs goes to large-scale developers who in turn continually act to increase these costs further. Seven out of the ten richest people in Britain are property speculators. They have added very little value to the economy but have extracted very large amounts of value. That is a straight transfer of wealth from citizens to the wealthy, and it is a very large scale transfer.

The second impact of this approach to housing is that it has trapped citizens in inflexible and onerous relationships to their homes. Because the cost of housing has become so high it now forms a very significant cost to households. High housing costs force people to work longer hours and reduce the capacity to alter relationships with employment. They trap people in homes where borrowing is high, reducing mobility and the flexibility needed with changing social situations. Again and again housing costs come up as the reason why forms of social change are difficult, with people responding to positive, innovative new ideas with 'yes please, but what about my mortgage?'. A house was never supposed to be a form of economic incarceration.

We need to reset our attitudes. In most countries a house is still primarily seen as a place for someone to live and not as a financial asset to be used for speculative purposes. We must change our policy approach to housing and seek to make it a source of collective wealth (where people live in good-quality secure homes spending a reasonable proportion of income on housing and without insecurity or anxiety) and not a source of commercial profit (where transferring as much land to private developers as possible is presented as a source of 'economic growth').

The means for doing this are straightforward – we need a massive increase in the supply of affordable, high-quality housing built to reflect the needs of those who live in them and not those who build them. This must be done in a way that controls house price rises or actively reduces house prices. This means that we need a major programme of building secure, high-quality public rented housing.

This can be done quickly and straightforwardly. Housing generates rent values so borrowing to build is simple. In the past borrowing has been done over short time-scales that force the rental value to be too high. We must borrow over mortgage-style periods of 30 years and more so that reasonable levels of rent are able to completely repay borrowing. This could be funded either from a National Investment Bank or a housing investment fund. But since the primary aim of the policy is to provide affordable rent, rent controls must be put in place and if for any reason the borrowing costs push the rental costs higher than the rent control threshold, public subsidy must be used to control prices.

There have been two problems with public sector housing in the past. One is that they tended to be managed inflexibly by local authorities, which were averse to allowing tenants any control over their home. Another more recent problem has been that smaller units of ownership (such as smaller housing associations) have tended to merge into bigger ones which have created ownership models which are too large and commercially focussed with sell-offs and underinvestment common outcomes.

To address this, the ownership of housing should be kept in the public sector, with mainly local authorities planning housing supply according to local need. However, the management of housing should be tenant-controlled in small units of local management. This local management should be in control of maintenance budgets to ensure constant investment in the houses to make sure that they do not deteriorate. Local management can also create a much more attractive service-orientated model of housing. For example, in other countries a 'concierge' system is common. A full-time, permanent manager is available to help with maintenance issue, to provide support for vulnerable tenants, to help deal with any disputes and so on. Subject to not seriously harming the integrity and value of the property or acting in an anti-social way, tenants should have the right to adapt and personalise their homes every bit as much as a private home-owner. Very long-term secure leases will be the norm.

As part of this process public policy should continually de-emphasise incentives to home ownership and must remove completely all subsidies to multiple home ownership. The value of housing assets should be taxed as capital gains and second homes should be fully taxed. A Land Value Tax would reduce speculation in land values and hoarding of land by developers and gradually lower the price of land for building. There should also be an assumption that public policy should work towards minimising the private rental sector by providing a higher-quality, better-value alternative. There are many innovative ways in which our attitude to housing can be changed. For example, mortgage-to-rent deals mean that people who own their homes could convert those homes to being publicly-owned but with reasonable rents and lifelong security of tenure. People who have been incentivised into home ownership which is against their best interests should have an exit option from a bad financial situation. Also the recently introduced restrictions on mortgage lending should help prevent people taking on mortgage commitments they are unable to repay.

This process will control house price rises and may well cause active reductions in house prices. This is to be welcomed; housing in Britain is greatly over-priced and high housing costs have mainly benefited financial

We need a massive increase in the supply of affordable, high-quality housing built to reflect the needs of those who live in them and not those who build them.

services companies, developers and speculators. We will never solve the housing problems we face if we don't correct the housing market.

However, this raises the issue of negative equity. Because of the corrupt and exploitative property and mortgage markets of the last 30 years almost everyone paid too high a price for their house and mortgages were offered at unrealistic and unsustainable rates. This made a lot of property and finance professionals very wealthy but left people in houses which were overpriced, over-mortgaged and in a financial position where their personal finances rested entirely on artificially low interest rates. There has already been one correction of the market (house prices declining to a more realistic value), which has currently left 77,000 Scots with houses worth less than their mortgage. However, this is a drop in the ocean of what is likely to happen when interest rates return to a more realistic level, putting hundreds of thousands of families into bankruptcy and/or negative equity.

We will have to deal with the impact of an over-mortgaged population living in overpriced houses eventually – the great housing con will catch up with us one way or another. The question is will the public pay for this to protect the wealth of financiers and speculators or to protect the interests of families? The Mortgage to Rent programme must be expanded to ensure that people who find themselves in negative equity can convert their mortgage to a rental arrangement – they have already lost the value of their house, they do not need to lose the right to live in their house or face bankruptcy. In the process of converting mortgages to rent, financial service companies which have profiteered from the rise in house prices must bear some of the brunt of the social cost of the decline – the days of the state underwriting the profits of the property industry need to come to an end. New rules mean that unaffordable mortgages are unlikely to be offered again.

Pretending that the housing situation in Scotland can continue along the trajectory set by the UK over recent decades will do us no good. The future will be different than the past; it is for us to ensure that future does not consists of hundreds of thousands of people homeless and bankrupt while the property industry ticks along like nothing happened but that we change the picture altogether.

In other aspects of our lives the picture has already changed. Access to the internet is now commonly described as being the fourth utility along with gas, water and electricity. It is an essential part of modern life across the globe and, alongside its communications role, accessing government and financial services now effectively depends on internet access. In Scotland 700,000 households still do not have internet access. Those without access include the most vulnerable and poorest in our society as well as certain rural communities.

An All-Of-Us-First approach dictates that all households have a right to access to a phone line and basic internet services. To make this a universal service it should be procured collectively by local authorities (who can negotiate cheap bulk deals), provided to every house and the cost added to the local tax. From that basic level of provision customers can then choose to pay for upgrades such as fast broadband and premium services such as films and sport, and being optional these services would be charged for by the providers. Having a duty to provide a basic service would, however, allow councils to reflect their citizens' wishes, for example as to whether WIFI should be freely available in town centres. It would also allow a rapid roll-out of online services of all types including new applications such as health monitoring, which aid the wellbeing and cohesion of the community and significantly reduce costs.

No wholesale nationalisation would be required or possible given the diversity of the industries. However, the duty to ensure service continuity to all households would require councils to have service contracts with, or directly employ, the engineers providing the telephone and internet link to homes just as this is done with gas, water and power engineers. There is no market in infrastructure development in telecoms in Scotland – it is the same small group of BT engineers who do all of it and that one corporation has won every single bid to provide infrastructure in Scotland. This should be recognised (and the myth of a competitive market being discarded) by progressively treating these as collectively controlled, leading to this facility being collectively owned.

This should encourage alternative technologies to be introduced, where appropriate, to provide a faster, cheaper internet provision to isolated communities. Existing government-backed programmes of working with the telecoms industry should continue to ensure the network architecture is improved to develop a fast, robust network throughout Scotland. This could be extended internationally, through participation in satellite and international data cables schemes, to ensure Scotland is a strong node within the world web.

Improving and expanding public transportation so that it is both affordable and accessible to everybody is fundamental to the idea of Common Weal. People and goods have to travel large distances in similar directions on a regular basis – why would we devise a system to meet this need that is anything other than the most efficient possible? And since transport organised on a public-collective basis (buses, trains and ships) is much more efficient and environmentally sustainable than transport organised on a private-individual basis (cars), how can it make sense not to invest in collective public transport? There are few other areas of life where the overwhelming efficiency of public-collective over private-individual is so clear.

Me-First politics mocks public transport, mostly viewing it as a second-rate option for those who can't afford a car. To prove its point, Me-First politics runs public transport for commercial profit with the minimum investment and in doing so creates a very poor quality but extremely expensive system (one of the most expensive in Europe) which really is a second-rate option. So yet again, Me-First politics seeks to show that All-Of-Us-First politics doesn't work by drilling a hole in the bottom of the boat, watching it sink and saying 'see – told you so'.

We cannot convince people to get out of the car and into public transport unless we make it easy and cheap for them to do so. The first step to doing so must be to re-nationalise ScotRail. The 'natural monopoly' of the railway service means that there is little incentive for private companies to reduce prices as they face little competition. Prices have grown well above wages, whilst company executives have received six-figure bumper salary increases. Bringing ScotRail back into public ownership does not even require the compensation that usually comes with re-nationalisation. The Scottish Government simply has to wait until the current contract on the franchise, which is held by FirstGroup, expires on the 31st of March 2015, and take up the contract as the new service provider. Not one penny has to be spent to buy the franchise back from shareholders as it has operated on a lease system.

The infrastructure, rolling stock and operating services need to be brought under one organisation to have a fully integrated and strategic direction for improving rail transport. This new system cannot just be top-down led, it must include government, worker and passenger representation to ensure the needs of the public as a whole are the first priority. It may also be necessary to have regular input from rural community leaders, environmentalists, green energy experts and business - transport cuts across all these groups and therefore we must balance the economy, the environment and the urban and rural population in our strategic outlook.

Prices needed to be significantly reduced to entice more people onto the rails, which will have to coincide with a major increase in manufacturing, maintenance and development of infrastructure to increase capacity. A sustainable national mutual company building rail infrastructure could create new jobs in manufacturing in Scotland. This new industry could be further boosted by an increasing use of freight on the railways, to reduce truck movement on the roads and increase efficiency. The shift from road to rail freight would in itself be a significant infrastructure challenge that would create jobs.

Expansion of the rail line to rural communities and the re-opening of derelict stations can, in combination with an effective rural industrial policy, be a key component in re-populating rural parts of Scotland and expanding business development beyond the central belt. Making more parts of Scotland's landscape cheap to get to and easily accessible would also be a big boost to Scotland's tourism industry, helping to realise Scotland's untapped potential in domestic tourism.

In inter-city rail links, upgrading including electrification and expansion is required. Rather than repeating the Edinburgh trams fiasco, public-public partnerships (PUPs) should be used for contracting rather than outsourcing. PUPs draw on relevant expertise from public sector practices in other countries and have been used extensively in water and electricity sectors in Latin America. They have been shown to be more efficient and of higher quality than PFI. Any model of investment that moves away from the UK system will help. Like so much of Me-First politics the UK system only works to protect corporate profits by passing costs on to passengers with no proper planning. It is incredibly inefficient and has created that perfect

A deal which says 'you have to suffer low wages but to help we'll give you cheap rubbish to eat' is not a good deal.

storm of poor quality and high prices. A properly-structured transport system will make much better use of investment.

Transport currently accounts for 23.7 per cent of Scotland's carbon emissions. Whilst a transition from road to rail is vital to change Scotland's travel habits, a shift from fossil fuels to green energy for road vehicles is also essential. There is already a Scottish roadmap to make vehicles carbon free. However, it concentrates on electric vehicles at a time when hydrogen is becoming recognised as the leading green transport fuel – it is cheaper, easier to produce and quicker to re-fuel. Scotland already has two hydrogen ferries and another is at the planning stage, hopefully to be Clyde-built. Aberdeen has the first UK fleet of Hydrogen buses (run by First Bus, but manufactured in Germany). Scottish bus companies could build these types of busses. Alexander Dennis, for example, is Scottish registered and claims to be the fastest growing bus manufacturer in Europe. There is also the option of building a national bus company around hydrogen buses. It could be used in all urban routes and given suitable refuelling points across the whole of Scotland.

All petrol stations could either generate hydrogen locally (for example in rural locations with little traffic) or deliver hydrogen through a pipe or from a tanker from a generating plant as would likely be necessary for motorway stations. Unlike electric cars, refuelling takes the same time as refuelling petrol vehicles. Hydrogen cars are being produced now, but it is likely these will only become widespread in around twelve years and the infrastructure needs to be put in place first. From an industrial point of view, installing refuelling points is the first goal for developing a hydrogen transport industry in Scotland. However, key components of vehicles such as various battery types could result in major manufacturing opportunities in Scotland as Scottish universities are among world leaders in this research. Other vehicle components could also be manufactured locally. Mass hydrogen storage will be necessary anyway and would boost Scotland's construction sector. Several smaller

Scottish electrolysis companies are world leaders and producing products and selling internationally, therefore the potential for hydrogen vehicles is evident.

For some rural areas, rail expansion is not cost effective. Therefore, community-owned bus and mini-bus services could be utilised, potentially with Government support or support from local community banks to get them started. For Scotland's islands, there is the potential for much greater investment in ferry services. Norway's publicly-owned ferry service, with its rugged coastal line comparative to Scotland's, could provide a model going forward.

This will require both action to increase rates of investment and action to reduce costs to the passenger. A good chunk of this will be raised by making public and collective transport a non-profit sector which means existing operators (all of which run at a profit) will not be extracting corporate profits. Long-term borrowing linked to the National Investment Bank will also significantly reduce the cost of investment – at the moment the cost of investing in infrastructure in Britain is just about the most expensive in the world because of the way it is paid for (generous amounts are added onto passenger fares on the basis of a faulty regulatory framework). This will enable some significant initial investment and reducing the cost of infrastructure development is key. It will take time for the financial models needed for a high-quality transport system at affordable fares to work. But it is essential we make it work.

While energy and heating should be taken into collective ownership and communications and transport will be a mixed system but with a much larger element owned collectively, food will of course remain an almost wholly privately owned part of our economy. However, that does not mean that food and food supply should be outside collective control.

Regulation and active policies to change and diversify food production and distribution would more effectively recognise that food is more important to society than any other market good. Food accounts for 25 to 30 per cent of greenhouse gas emissions and agriculture globally is a major driver of habitat and biodiversity loss, so a shift towards climate-smart agro-ecological production methods and sustainable diets would be integral to food policy.

It would also make clear that food is both a driver of change (economically, environmentally and socially) and a sign of change (a Common Weal Scotland will be identifiable by people eating better and food being produced more sensitively).

A food policy should create a move towards a much more mixed economy of food processing, distribution, retailing and catering. Mutual institutions such as food buying co-operatives and community food hubs would create a focus for ethical collective sourcing, community catering, urban farming and local employment. Community food hubs would offer an alternative to food banks, providing food credit in emergencies.

The current 'big box' model of multiple retailers would coexist with a range of direct sourcing models connecting communities to farmers and farmers co-operatives in Scotland and across the world.

It would encourage much more localised food economies, discourage cheap processed food and put more emphasis on quality and nutrition than on corporate profit in all policies that affect food production and consumption. As a Common Weal Scotland becomes more wealthy and we tackle poverty and inequality, paying a little more for food will become normal – and beneficial. The low wages and insecure employment conditions in the catering and retail sector would change, with food work being more highly valued with food workers expected to be skilled and knowledgeable about health and provenance. In fact, since food production is an important industry in Scotland, slightly higher food prices over time will boost the economy and actually create the higher wealth to absorb costs.

Cheap, processed foods are bad for our health and every bit as bad for our economy. Low-quality, low-nutrition, highly-processed foods do not only directly harm our health and wellbeing, they undermine our economy and cost us enormously in what we pay to tackle the health impacts of obesity and heart disease. A deal which says 'you have to suffer low wages but to help we'll give you cheap rubbish to eat' is not a good deal. The deal we want is a high-wage economy where we can afford to eat decent food.

Our food production can then become a process that invests in our natural capital rather than destroying it. It will enhance the environment, biodiversity and land management, which in turn will sustain the environment in which farming can thrive. Farming will not take place only in an industrialised environment but will accommodate a peopled, wooded landscape, which provides a habitat for the wildlife that creates a sustainable land. There would be a transformation in ownership patterns with many more small farms, specialist producers and local retailers. Cooperative and mutual ownership of food production and distribution would be normal – whether that is better provision of allotments, cooperative farming or community-owned bakers, greengrocers and butchers.

There would also be a well-developed 'not for profit' sector geared to good clean and fair food – and the whole sector would be paying a living wage. Advocacy for farm animals is well-developed and welcomed by farmers as part of the partnership between farmers and public. Farming is a respected profession, with a continuing professional development framework and women are well-represented throughout the food and farming sector. This model will create a lot more employment.

Perhaps above all, in a Common Weal Scotland food will no longer be a class issue. In Scotland today eating healthy food is seen as a middle-class 'thing'; promoting good food to working class people is treated almost as a pointless curiosity not linked to their lives. Food would be seen as a way of creating social capital, improving health but just as importantly improving self respect and self-confidence. Food would be embedded into what we teach our children, eating would be a family and social activity, cooking would be a universal skill. Our consumption patterns would be shaped by the greater confidence this produced with people choosing good food they know how to cook rather than being driven by lack of self confidence into reheating bad food marketed as easy and effort-free.

Much of the problem stems from the capture of the food production and distribution by big commercial interests, which then drove a rapid intensification of farming. It is assumed that much of the gain from that intensification has gone to farmers and consumers; in fact much more of the gain has gone to large commercial processors and supermarkets and it is they that have shaped the food landscape we have. Tackling the dominance of these monopoly players is key and an industrial policy is a major step to achieve that. Greater regulation of the industry to prevent practices that are profitable but harmful to health and wellbeing is necessary. It may also be necessary to use tax incentives to reduce the competitiveness of cheap, bad processed foods. It will certainly be necessary to support high streets, local shopping and independent suppliers if we are to re-localise food distribution.

We need to move from a common agricultural policy towards a common food policy, changing the focus from 'what is good for our existing big producers' to 'what is good for the whole system of food production, distribution and consumption'. Subsidies must then be realigned with the aims of that policy. The role of local authorities and public agencies in creating a mixed food economy is crucial, not least in how they use procurement when buying food and catering. It will also include a wide-ranging and inclusive national dialogue that involves civil society, academics, ecologists, farmers, medical professions and politicians.

To stimulate independent food production and processing we need to create a system of patient investment finance through a national investment bank. This should help not only many more small- and medium-scale farmers but also many small- and medium-scale processors such as artisan bakers, microbreweries, local butchers and so on.

And we need access to more land – which opens up another area of shared interest. Land ownership and use in Scotland is now universally recognised as failing.

Fewer than one thousand people own over half of Scotland's land. Scotland has the most concentrated land ownership in the whole of Europe. If we are to become a more equal nation that uses its resources to the benefit of everyone, we need a much more equitable distribution of land. But we also need land reform for immediate economic reasons – large swathes of land which is kept unproductive so it can be traded as a speculative asset (perhaps the primary aim of much of Scotland's land ownership) simply strips Scotland of its access to its own valuable natural assets. This also has the effect of making proper rural development virtually impossible in large areas of Scotland.

Land owners often have little interest in local development because they increase their vast (usually inherited) wealth simply from the rising price of land and property and, subsequently, rents. This is a classic case of wealth extraction; rather than use the wealth of the land to build and create more wealth for everyone, the land is simply used to extract more wealth for the owners by the least productive means possible. The current tax system perpetuates that gross injustice. For example, if the general public pay through taxation to build a new train line that is built next to a large landowner, his land will immediately increase in value as a result. The landowner will not be taxed on that increase in value, and therefore his wealth increases without doing or contributing anything.

Because land value has increased at a greater rate than other investment, it is actually against the interests of a landowner to have tenants or production on his land as it drops the value. This is one of the main reasons why Scotland has massive areas of unproductive land which has the characteristics of a desert – no biodiversity, no shrub or tree life, poor soil and so on. This harms food production, rural economic development, the emergence of new industries like biomass farming, house-building and so on.

Therefore, we need radical land reform to challenge the undemocratic and unjust system of land ownership we currently have. First, we need to get the land into the hands of the local people who will make use of it. We need to give tenant farmers a right to buy their farms from the lairds that own them. Tenant farmers are often scared to speak out in case they are kicked off the land, yet they do all the work on the farm whilst the lairds take the profits. Second, we need to also make community buy-outs much easier so, for example, rural communities can build affordable social housing to keep young people in the area and, thus, keep alive the post offices, local shops and farms that are fundamental to the survival of rural communities.

Intertwined with this is a need for radical decentralisation of planning permission, so that for example, North-Ayrshire Council isn't making decisions over whether to build a home on the Island Bute. Local communities have to be able to control planning, not distant councils that are not part of the community and, in the case of Argyll and Bute, are not even on the same land mass.

Finally, we must use a Land Value Tax to bring down the price of land, making it easier for communities to buy it, lessening the desirability for wealthy land-owners to keep hold of it and bringing in a significant amount of revenue for the public purse in the process. The benefit of this is that it reduces the disincentive for investment in new buildings as property is taxed as part of the land rather than as property itself. Secondly, it recognises that the value of land is often not intrinsic, i.e. it is determined by wider factors than the land itself, and therefore the wider community should benefit from increases in land value too. Third, Land Value Tax is very hard to avoid. As long as there is a fully-functioning land information system of ownership, occupation, land use and land values the state can easily tax land owners.

A Common Weal Scotland must be built on shared foundations that benefit us all and underpin our society, not through exploitation but through mutual benefit.

Chapter Six

WORKING LIFE

Work should make our lives richer, not poorer

Create real industrial democracy with strong trade-unions.
Involve workers in the running of businesses.
Enshrine better rights for working people.
Take health and safety protection seriously.
Work better, work less with a 30-hour week.

The biggest and most passionate debate in Britain is about work; it's just that this debate takes place almost wholly outside politics. No matter where you go in Scotland you will find people talking about work – their hope for a better job, a more rewarding job, better pay, more time for family life, more respect, more training, more scope for progress.

This is not surprising; work is an incredibly large part of our lives. And yet public policy attitudes towards work are astoundingly narrow, reaching little beyond how to reduce unemployment and how to make life as easy as possible for employers. Me-First economics requires that low-pay corporations are able to access large pools of workers who can be made to accept the low-pay, low-skill jobs they seek to fill. It is also expected that all the negative social and economic costs of this system should be passed on to the public, that the commitment of employer to employee should be virtually non-existent and that the aim of regulation is to achieve these outcomes while allowing the corporation to make the maximum profit on the basis of this low-pay employment.

In practice, this means that Britain has a degraded labour market. It has the second lowest level of industrial democracy among 28 European Union countries – only Lithuania is worse. Giving workers no democratic power in the workplace has underpinned the deterioration in the quality of working life experienced by British workers. It has led to Britain having the second lowest pay among advanced economies, the third longest working hours (and fewest holidays) in Europe and one of the least secure working conditions of workers anywhere in Europe. Tax credits are a massive state subsidy to low-pay corporations who can pay workers a wage below that which would be sufficient to survive on because the taxpayer picks up the difference. Likewise, the massive scale of underemployment (people who work insecure hours that don't provide enough work to earn a living wage) is paid for by the benefits system. It is possible to see much of that system as in effect being a cash transfer to low-pay, low-security employers.

Along with this goes widespread deskilling and deregulation. Since people with skills need to be paid better wages the UK economy has, through management practice and its approach to investing in technology, sought to centralise or automate the skilled part of the work so wages and hours can be depressed further. The practices of zero-hour contracts (a process not a long way away from making people wait by the side of the road each morning to find out if they can get any hours of work), unpaid internships, forced labour (through benefit sanctions) and negligible health and safety inspections for many workers are simply logical conclusions of this approach to work.

So let us remind ourselves of that crucial principle of All-Of-Us-First economics; it is work that creates wealth. The Me-First economist may claim that it is 'economic growth' that creates jobs hence it is growth that creates wealth. But if that were true, the last 20 years of economic growth would have created widespread wealth. In fact, it has created widespread poverty. It is not the simple act of total profit in the economy increasing that creates national wealth but how and where that wealth is created. If it is based on high-skill and high-productivity, that does indeed create the kinds of jobs that create wealth. If it is based on speculation and profiteering it does quite the opposite. Our national wealth relies on good work.

But it is not only our national wealth that relies on good work but also our national wellbeing. The attributes of the UK economy have a clear, negative effective on health, wellbeing and family life. The insecurity which is built into the UK's labour laws means that large proportions of the population are at constant risk of short-notice redundancy or, even if in contracted labour, no certainty of any income at all in any given week. This is a work environment in which fear of losing a job is the primary concern; obedience is often seen as the only response to insecurity. The low levels of pay and low worker protection mean that long hours and stress and anxiety are routine. The long hours mean that many workers have little time for their families or themselves, which creates relationship stress, unhappiness, family breakdown and a general inability to participate in society.

This should be a matter of national outrage. Instead it is treated as a dirty secret with few politicians even willing to raise the issue of whether the quality of working lives should form a part of national political debate. But it must.

If Scotland is to be a democracy in any meaningful sense then the priorities of citizens must set the foundations of political debate. If the priorities of citizens were taken seriously, the quality and nature of work would be one of the most important political debates we would be having.

So what do people say they want from work? There are really three elements; security, respect and balance. It is interesting when you ask people (as opposed to economists or employers) what it is they want from their work they do not emphasise wealth. People tend to say that what they want from their work is not the theoretical chance of high income but rather the certainty of economic security. It is not the chance to be rich but the certainty of not being poor that people want. If they can be assured that each month they can live a fulfilling life and at the end of the month they can pay the bills, then that is what most people define as their economic ambition. Aspiration is what Me-First economists think people want; what people say they want is security.

Respect is as important as reward. It is the concept of 'meaningful work' that keeps coming up when people are asked. They want two kinds of respect. First they want the respect of employers and colleagues, the sense that they are not unskilled drones but people with talent who are capable, can be trusted and have personal attributes to bring to the workplace which make them valuable and valued. The second is self-respect; the sense that when you get up in the morning you are going to do something that is worthwhile, that makes you feel that your contribution is important and that your days are not a meaningless waste of time. This is why caring professions, even where they are lower paid and often have long hours and a lot of stress, are seen as much more rewarding by the people who fill those jobs than people in routine sales work – even if it pays better.

Finally, people want balance. Work is important to self-worth – it is interesting that people who for whatever reason are unable to take paid work are happier and more fulfilled if they are able to do unpaid work. So it is very far from the right-wing tabloid view that ordinary people are some sort of natural shirkers who would skive off work any time they could and must be compelled through either the bribery of high pay or the fear of poverty.

We have to reverse Britain's terrible stewardship of working life. The first and most important step towards that is to create a real, active industrial democracy.

People want to work; it makes them feel part of society. But there is a balance; they want to feel alive too. Time with family is simply not taken seriously in Britain. Neither is recreation (here meant in the original sense of 'to re-create yourself as a person through learning, participation, activity and entertainment'). People want time to realise themselves as people. They do not get it in Britain.

We have to reverse Britain's terrible stewardship of working life. The first and most important step towards that is to create a real, active industrial democracy. Industrial democracy is about the ability for workers to have some say and some control in the workplace and to be able to work with employers to further their interests. Effective industrial democracy is not about conflict or fighting but about collective working. There inevitably will be disputes and disagreements from time to time but an effective system of industrial democracy begins from an awareness from both parties (employers and employees) that in fact their interests are often broadly shared.

Creating industrial democracy in Scotland will have to begin by addressing the toxic legacy of the UK's political attitude to trade unions and workers' rights. This is not just a matter of low levels of worker protection and anti-trade union legislation but the way Westminster has portrayed industrial relations as always a matter of conflict. The standard view of industrial democracy in British politics is of a running battle between employers and employees whose interests are always in opposition – and that it is the responsibility of government to favour the interests of employers (for the economic benefit of all, of course).

This is not how industrial democracy is seen in other countries. Of course, there will occasionally be disputes and of course sometimes the interests of employers and employees will differ and compromise will be required. But in many neighbouring countries workers are seen not only as 'hired help' but as fundamental partners in the success of businesses. It is recognised that if the skills and knowledge of workers can be used to improve the running of the company it creates productivity improvement and high rates of innovation. These countries routinely accept that positive working conditions benefit all and employers and employees alike support widespread collective bargaining of pay and conditions – and hence strong trade unions. They recognise that workers need to be treated well if they are to contribute well and so workers' rights (including protecting time off) are enshrined. And they recognise that workers have very valuable job knowledge, which can be used to improve the way the company is run – so they are included in the governance of enterprises.

What is important in all of this is not just that there is legislation that enshrines and encourages these behaviours and attitudes but that these behaviours and attitudes are seen as ones which should be encouraged. That is where we must begin; by creating a system of industrial democracy, which is supported by all sides, all of which (employers, employee, shareholder, politician, the public) understand the mutual benefits and want to work together to achieve them.

The mutual benefits are significant. In most advanced economies a very large proportion of innovation is employee innovation. When industrial democracy is working an individual employee can notice that there is a better way to do something ('if we turned that conveyor belt round the other way we could get twice as many people on it and double production....') and is then able to present that idea to a governance system which includes workers. Good ideas are then willingly adopted by boards and managers. When it isn't working, two people on minimum wage and zero-hour contracts also realise that the conveyor belt is running the wrong way. But since they have absolutely no stake in the success of the company, they go home disillusioned, not believing their ideas matter anyway.

Higher rates of innovation create productivity improvement. So do better terms and conditions – hour-for-hour worked an employee who is not exhausted and demoralised produces more. Working relations that create secure, long-term working relationships creates a shared interest in making the business work well and for the long term. Employees involved in governance tend to make decisions that favour long-term investment in the enterprise and in particular investment in skills and training.

This balances the interests of shareholders who may favour short-term profit. Employees bring a different and complementary knowledge to governance, enhancing what managers bring. And employee governance tends to 'anchor' enterprises into the economy, discouraging equity sales and take-over by multinationals.

Indeed, so embedded is this positive view of industrial democracy in other economies that shareholders openly expect employee involvement in governance. One major shareholder in Volkswagen (one third of the board of management of which is elected by employees) explained that without employee involvement in running the company the Board would have little or no knowledge about what was happening on its own shop floor. In turn, employees recently persuaded the Board to pass company rules that prevented any employee from using work phones or email between 7pm and 9am because it was impacting negatively on family life. They also recently reigned in the salary of the chief executive, which was felt to be rising too fast in comparison to other workers. Suffice to say, Volkswagen is a very successful company.

In Britain, an academic study recently showed that companies that are unionised are 20 per cent more productive than equivalent companies which are not. Another recent study showed that mutual and cooperative businesses (where employees not only help govern but also own the enterprise) are even more successful economically. Across a full range of measures of economic and social performance, all the countries in the top half for performance are also in the top half of the table for industrial democracy – and all the countries with the lowest economic and social performance come from the bottom half of the league table on industrial democracy.

If we can start from a shared understanding of this truth – that industrial democracy is good for everyone – we can start to build a system that benefits everyone.

This must begin with strong trade unions and widespread collective bargaining coverage. It is important to have a living wage and to pursue an industrial policy which rebalances the economy towards high-pay. This will end the worst of the low-pay problems and work towards a better labour market (see above and below), but it alone will not reduce pay inequality and 'compress' wage levels to create a more equal society. That requires workers to be able to negotiate a fairer proportion of the benefits of economic growth so that more of that growth goes to wage growth and less to profits which benefit only the small number of people who own large enterprises. In the

UK, we have about 20 per cent of workers covered by collective bargaining; in Denmark it is well over 80 per cent.

Trade unions are important because otherwise workers are left individually (or even collectively but without support) to negotiate pay and conditions and they are simply not properly equipped or prepared to negotiate successfully. Asymmetrical negotiation, where one side is much stronger than the other, is a large part of how the UK has become so unequal in pay and why working conditions have declined so quickly. The aim should be to unionise as widely as possible. However, since the aim should be to seek collective bargaining at an industry sector level, trade unions should lead in negotiating for the workforces in sectors even where there are lower levels of trade union involvement. Creating fair, consistent sector-level agreements help all enterprises to compete from an equal footing.

The second step towards achieving industrial democracy is to make sure that workplace regulation properly protects the interests of workers. This covers everything from job security to health and safety to pay and conditions (such as statutory rights to maternity and paternity leave). It also requires legislation, which regulates trade unions and actively promotes widespread trade union membership and the ability of unions to represent the interests of workers fairly and effectively. Some of the sorts of conditions that should be put in place will be considered under the need to reduce working hours and the need to create social security (both below).

The third step towards achieving proper industrial democracy is to create worker involvement in governance. This is not about workers being put on the management boards of companies to argue about pay and conditions – as has been made clear above it is through trade unions that these issues should be resolved. Appointing workers to boards or involving them in governance in other ways is not a substitute for this and must not be seen as a 'work-around' way to undermine collective bargaining. It is about helping workers to help enterprises be better and to help employers and owners to better understand the issues facing their employees. It gives workers access to influence and shape the strategic direction of an enterprise.

In both Germany and Denmark any company over a certain threshold of employees (500 in the case of Denmark) is obliged to offer at least a third of the places on its board of management for worker representatives elected from within the workforce. Smaller companies also have a responsibility to allow employees to elect members onto governing bodies but have a lower threshold. For multinational companies or companies who are headquartered outside Scotland, workers should have the right to elect members to sit on whatever is the highest level of governance for that corporation in that country. Employees on boards are full members of that board, with exactly the same rights to see company accounts, management information and any other information pertinent to the running of the business. This is known as Board Level Employee Representation (sometimes called BLER for short) and the employees elected to boards are known as employee directors, who are mandated by workers from the shop floor to make proposals and report back on board business.

BLER covers the role of employees in running companies at the boardroom level. But there is also a need to have more collegiate running of the shop floor. This is the role of cooperation committees. These are committees usually made up half of worker representations and half of management representation. They are organised on the basis of specific shop floors – one company that manufactured at different sites would have different cooperation committees for each. These deal with the operating issues at a given site; anything from advising on the use of new technology to training and facilities (but again, these do not negotiate terms and conditions).

So trade unions work with employers to create fair terms and conditions for all workers, regulation and legislation protects the fundamental interests of workers, employee-directors help to shape the overall running of an enterprise and workplace coordinating committees help to run each shop floor efficiently and effectively.

To make all of this work well from where we are will require a significant investment in effort, training and support. Everyone involved must have support in learning and developing their new roles and in understanding the different relationships in the workplace that must result. The benefits that come to everyone from getting this right will more than repay the investment of effort made.

Part of the deregulation of the workplace, which came along with the attacks on industrial democracy was a weakening of occupational health and safety protection. Among the 30 OECD economies, the UK is now the 20th worst nation for health and safety. Both the occurrence of work-related accidents and the health impacts of work practices (for example, asbestosis which

Overwork creates significant economic, social and psychological harm. To create a Common Weal economy we must try to create the sort of working culture they have in Europe's most successful economies where working better is the aim, not working longer.

is very often a result of the workplace but which may not be picked up for many years) are far too high. The health and wellbeing of workers must be given top priority.

So there should be a Scottish Occupational Health and Safety Agency to monitor and enforce the best standards of occupational protections. The Agency should use the precautionary principle – if in doubt, don't take risks with people's lives. This means, for example, using the most internationally up to date prescribed occupational disease lists, toxics use reduction approaches, control of job-related stress and establishing whistle-blower hotlines, support and protection.

Worker and community health and safety centres across Scotland should also be established to advise employees about prevention and detection of disease and injury and to provide support for victims. There should be better support for training and development of health and safety reps in the workplace. Profit is never worth the price of a dead worker and none of us should face risk of harm while going about our jobs.

But the debate about work is bigger than simply being about improving the quality of the work we have; it is also about balancing the volume of work we have with the lives we hope to live. In Britain workers work among the longest hours in Europe and have the fewest holidays. This has many damaging effects – and they're seldom discussed by politicians. The economic impacts of overwork include diminished productivity, absenteeism and a knock-on cost for welfare. Workers who work long hours become exhausted and demoralised and this affects the quality of their work. They are both less able to perform well and less motivated to try. This also leads to absenteeism where both exhaustion and demoralisation lead to health issues which cause lost days of work. The net effect adds to the overall problem of low-pay, low-productivity employment in Scotland which in turn leads to significant costs for the benefit system.

The social impacts of overwork include impact on family life, poorer quality of service for customers from exhausted staff, a damaging emphasis on constant consumption, a low level of civic participation and problems of gender inequality. If you are being treated by an exhausted nurse, if you are having electrical work done by an over-worked electrician, if you are being served by a stressed waiter, your experience of life deteriorates. When we have no time in our lives we are pushed to replace the lost time through over-consumption of processed foods, disposable goods, services we don't really need and products that make us think we feel better such as alcohol, tobacco, fatty foods and 'retail therapy'. Civic participation is one of the important roles of citizenship which takes a significant hit; people don't feel they have time to participate, to volunteer, to get involved in community, to join groups and to strengthen public life. The impacts of long working hours tend to impact particularly on woman who often have to cope with both longer hours and family caring responsibilities.

But it is time with family and time for recreation, which have been harmed most by the long-hours culture. Getting home just in time to see your children go to bed, working weekends and anti-social hours, being unable to take time off during school holidays and being tired and irritable when we do have time with family are all symptoms which harm public wellbeing. In place of recreation (a process of changing ourselves, stimulating our minds and realising our hopes through activity and participation) we have passive consumption of instantly forgettable commercial entertainment. It is hobbies, pastimes, engaging with creativity and socialising which are most damaged by long working. This, of course, leads to the psychological impacts of overwork including stress, ill-health and low levels of happiness. There are also many environmental impacts of overwork resulting from the power consumption of offices and workplaces that are open for long periods of time, the impact of commuting and the over-consumption of processed foods.

Overwork creates significant economic, social and psychological harm. To create a Common Weal economy we must try to create the sort of working culture they have in Europe's most successful economies where working better is the aim, not working longer - and where happiness and family life are not secondary issues.

Even in the economy that Scotland has just now, if we reduced our working hours we would be able to redistribute the work that we have more evenly. In fact, if we moved to a 30-hour working week we would create enough new jobs to achieve full employment with no-one unemployed. Most people would be able to work four-day weeks, though flexibility would mean that people might choose school hour contracts (9.30 until 3 so work can fit around childcare) or other forms of working arrangements.

Of course there are challenges that must be overcome to get there, especially to ensure that economic changes happen so people aren't worse off because of working fewer hours. A range of proposals for how to move to a high-pay economy ha been outlined above and more will be discussed below. We will need to deal with overpriced housing and excessive housing debt, which traps people into needing to work long hours; this too has been looked at above. We also need to integrate many other policy areas more effectively like food and energy policy, which can create security and affordability.

These are all needed to put in place a ten-year phased plan to move to the 30-hour week. This would involve four phases: in years one to three new public-sector jobs and new contracts would go on to a 30-hour week; in years three to five a 40-hour legal limit for all workers would be introduced and all public-sector will be on at least 35 hour week contracts; in years five to ten all employees will be offered a 30-hour week and there will be five years worth of data to assess effectiveness; and in years 10 and beyond almost all workers should be on a 30-hour week contract with a 35-hour legal limit as skills gaps should have been filled by increased training and employment by then.

A Common Weal Scotland is built by – and on – work. Work makes us wealthy and feel good about ourselves – and it drives many of the improvements in our economy.

Chapter Seven

SOCIAL SECURITY

We can build a society based on security, not anxiety

Make work pay by introducing a Living Wage.

Ensure guaranteed income in employment contracts.

Integrate social security with economy and work policies to make pay more equal.

Reduce housing costs to make housing affordable.

Introduce a citizen's Income to provide financial security for all.

Help people with additional needs through proper financial support.

What is our collective responsibility to those who are in a less fortunate position than others? Are we a nation that measures itself on the basis of how we treat the weakest in our society (as Greek philosopher Aristotle urged)? Or are we a nation that measures itself according to how the most powerful are doing (as Margaret Thatcher insisted we must)?

This is a fundamental question. Are we a society that creates 'safety nets' to help catch those who 'fall off the end' of society (usually because they have lost work, have an onerous caring responsibility, have a health problem or have grown old) or do we want to make sure that no-one falls 'off the end' of society – because society does not 'end'? In the former version of society we provide just enough public and private 'charity' to prevent people starving or freezing to death if they lose their income (or in modern Britain, if their income isn't enough to survive on). In the latter we create systems that prevent people needing charity in the first place.

The language that has been used in this debate is telling. We used to use 'welfare' to describe the whole post-war political settlement which included the NHS, public housing, nationalised industries and a strong system of public insurance against loss of work or ill health (this is the welfare state). Social security was a part of that welfare state that dealt with those who for whatever reason did not have enough income to survive. Now Me-First opponents of the welfare state have adopted the American usage of welfare, a derogatory term which is associated with the meaning 'giving money to useless people'. We call the money given 'benefits', as if a political and economic system that leaves you in poverty and then offers you a minimal level of charity is some-how beneficial to you.

The language underlines the philosophy of 'welfare' politics – that social protection from unemployment and ill health should be as low as possible to make people's lives as miserable as possible that they will want to get back into work as quickly as possible and on whatever terms are offered by the market. This Me-First approach to citizenry believes that, given the choice, people will avoid work and 'live on benefits'. In this view the only way to discipline you inherently lazy, unproductive citizens is to discipline you through anxiety. The fear of the suffering which comes with losing work or being unable to work through ill-health in Britain must be so great that no-one would choose to live like that. There is even a widely-held Me-First belief that social protection must follow a 'worse than the worst' rule – whatever the very worst employer that can be found anywhere in the country pays, 'welfare' must be worse than that. If it isn't, how will anyone ever be found to fill that job? It is a system that is designed almost explicitly to punish the poor and force them into the low-est paid jobs available. It is also a system that is designed to prevent people in poor-quality, low-security employment getting ideas above themselves (like a Living Wage). The idea that people may have any goals or aims towards a bet-ter career or the hope of starting a business are not even considered. Me-First politics thinks fear is the only weapon that can be used to deal with the 'lazy' poor (whilst greed works much better as a motivator for the already rich).

There is another way to approach the relationship of those in the weakest social position. An All-Of-Us-First view believes that, as members of our society, we have a responsibility to ensure a decent standard of living for all of our neighbours, no matter what ill-fortune befalls them. It believes that being employed by a badly-managed business that goes bankrupt, or having a loved one that falls seriously ill and requires you to provide full-time care, or that getting too old to work are not your fault and that you should not be made to suffer as a result. But it also believes that if we want to build a good economy then when citizens lose work they must be able to be in a position to try and find good, productive employment or to start a business or whatever is most likely to contribute to an effective economy. All of this means that we need to stop using the failed motiva-tors of anxiety and fear and start emphasising the motivator of security and self-confidence.

For this reason we should return to using the language of 'social security'. We should design the social security system so that we can all plan our future economic and social contribution to Scotland not from a position of fear but of confidence. We do not need a system that demoralises people and then bullies them into meaningless low-pay work. We need people to have a solid foundation for their lives so that they can help build a strong and productive economy and not simply be used as raw materials for a poor-quality, exploitative economy.

A system that emphasised social security would therefore look at all the aspects that make people insecure and find ways to replace anxiety with confidence. Once again, this is not a policy that can be fixed by finding one big 'magic button' and pressing it. It must work through the problem and fix it bit by bit.

The first step in this process is to address the problem of acute low pay. It simply cannot be acceptable in 21st Century Scotland that someone can work a 40-hour week and still not have sufficient income to live independently. We do not need to take social security and make it as bad as the worst possible job but rather we have to create a decent level of social security and make sure that no paid employment falls below that standard. The current system allows employers to pay a wage that can't be lived on and then let the public purse pick up the cost of keeping that person alive. It is a direct cash subsidy to the profit of low-pay employers, many of which are large multinational companies that are extremely profitable.

So we need a Living Wage. A Living Wage is a sum calculated at a rate which pays enough per hour for someone to earn enough in full-time work to live independently. Simply moving from a Minimum Wage (currently £6.31 per hour) to a Living Wage (currently £7.65 per hour) would save a quarter of a billion pounds in tax credits, much of which subsidises companies like Tesco. It would also set a clear statement of values – work must pay fairly and fairly must mean that someone who works can live independently on their income.

Most big employers can comfortably absorb the costs of a Living Wage – indeed, in most neighbouring countries they already do. Researchers have shown that if the big supermarkets chose to pass on all of the extra cost to consumers it would barely raise the price of groceries at all and would certainly be less of a burden than what we currently pay in tax credits. At the moment,

We should design the social security system so that we can all plan our future economic and social contribution to Scotland not from a position of fear but of confidence.

many smaller businesses in low-margin sectors like tourism and hospitality might struggle to pay a Living Wage so part of the £250 million saved from working tax credits would be used to subsidise those employers (for example through a targeted National Insurance cut). In time we need to create an economy where every employer pays a Living Wage without subsidy. We certainly need to move away from a system where someone working full time still faces the stigma of requiring benefit payments to survive.

The second step is to turn security of hourly pay into security of income. Much has been made by advocates of a Me-First economy of the need for 'flexibility'. This, they claim, is something that is wanted by both employers and employees – and so Zero-Hour Contracts (where people do not know if they will have any hours of work in any given week) are presented as a benefit to all. This view of the labour market is not borne out by research; in fact, almost all of the 'flexibility' in the labour market is employer flexibility ('I want to pay you only when I need to and have no further responsibility to you as an employer') and very little is employee flexibility ('I need a contract which gets me home reliably and on time for the kids coming home from school').

It is certainly the case that flexibility in working patterns is a feature of the modern economy and should be supported. But there is a difference between flexibility in working patterns and insecurity of income. Anyone in contracted employment should have a guaranteed monthly minimum income from employment. It should be possible to organise those working hours in any mutually agreeable way and it should be possible to add to those minimum working hours – but it should not be possible to reduce those number of working hours. To avoid abuse of this system any employee who regularly works more hours per month than their contract states should have the right to see their contracted hours increase in line with the hours actually worked.

At this stage we have addressed the problem of acute low pay (those who can't earn enough to survive as a result of a low hourly wage rate) and income insecurity (those who don't know if they will earn enough because they don't know if they'll get sufficient hours). Another problem is underemployment – people who can't get enough hours of work. We have already seen above how changing working patterns and moving away from endemic long hours will create the conditions that will offer the chance of full employment to all.

The next problem to deal with is chronic low pay – not those whose salary is so low that it is insufficient to survive on but those above and just above that threshold who might be able to manage a basic level of subsistence but who are still constantly financially stressed or who are unable to support a family. In the UK we pay tax credits for low pay to a remarkable proportion of the population. In fact, more than half of all adults in Scotland pay less in tax (because they are low paid) than they receive in benefits and services. Imagine you lined up 100 people to represent all the households in Scotland and made them stand from poorest to richest. Imagine that you started to walk up the line from the poorest to the richest. When you reach the 55th person their household receives 40 per cent of its total income from cash benefits (this does not include the value of public services used, only direct cash payments). Fifty four people in that line before them are poorer. By the time you get to the 65th person they're still getting 22 per cent of their income from cash benefits. And by the time you reach the 75th person (so three quarters of every household in Scotland earns less than this person), even that household is receiving 13 per cent of their income in cash benefits.

It cannot be repeated enough; we have a chronic low-pay economy. And since by far the best way to deal with social security payments is not to need them, the next step is essential; we need to move to a high-pay economy. It is here that social security policy must be fully integrated with the industrial policy and the industrial democracy policy. We have already seen how favouring a different kind of economy and making employees stakeholders in the economy by giving them some economic power will move us towards a high-pay economy with much lower levels of inequality. This is essential in creating social security – and social security is essential to creating a high-pay economy. If we have secure citizens ready to contribute to the economy that will make for a much better economy than demoralised, anxious citizens being forced to stack shelves for poverty wages.

Above all, we must integrate social security policy with all the range of policies that compress pay scales and make people wealthier.

The next problem we have to deal with is housing. As we have seen, the balance between public expenditure on building houses and paying housing benefit has shifted from 80:20 thirty years ago to 5:95 now. House prices and rents have got out of control, this cost has been passed to the public to meet through housing benefit and then housing benefit has flooded the rental market helping to contribute to the rising house prices. For the time being we should retain a specific payment to help with housing costs, but this must be completely integrated with housing policy. The aim should be to make sure there are enough affordable housing options that immediately reduces housing benefit bills and then, over time, we create a system of housing and high-pay employment that means people do not need special housing payments. We have already seen how we should use housing policy rapidly to increase supply and so decrease housing costs. This must be integrated at all stages with social security policy.

The next step is to design a social security system that really does focus on security, but does it while holding to the fundamental principles of Common Weal. As a reminder, the way to make the poor secure is not to separate them from the rest of society and treat them differently but rather to design systems in which everyone is included. This is especially the case where people may move in and out of poverty conditions if they lose work and then find a new job because each time they join a different 'queue' (the one for people without work who need help and the one for people who are in low pay work and need help) they face all sorts of perverse 'traps' like becoming poorer for working longer because cash benefits fall faster than wages rise.

There is a simple and elegant way to address all these problems and many more. It is called a Citizen's Income (sometimes known as a Basic Income or a Citizen's Basic Income). This is a payment that is made to every single citizen whether they are in work or not and provides a sum which is enough to support a basic level of life. It can be created immediately in a cost-neutral manner (I.e. no more expensive than the existing payments it would replace). To create a three-tier payment (one for children, one for 18-65 year-olds and one for those over 65) all we have to do is to take Jobseekers Allowance and other unemployment benefits, tax allowances for those in work, the pension for those who are retired, tax credits and child benefit and use that income to create a system of universal Citizen's Income. In this very basic system every adult of working age would receive a monthly or weekly payment equivalent to Jobseekers Allowance and every adult over the age of 65 would receive an enhanced Citizen's Income equivalent to the state pension (groups like carers might also receive the enhanced version).

This would be cost neutral for both the citizen and for public finances. However it has some immediate beneficial effects. Firstly, there is no need for any form of means testing so the system is much more efficient and reaches everyone. Secondly, it sends out a strong message about the need to create security for all in a Common Weal Scotland. While it might be superficial, people in insecure work will receive a payment that lets them know they have a support system behind them if anything goes wrong – and it will be exactly the same support system that everyone else receives.

But the biggest immediate benefit comes from overcoming what is known as the 'withdrawal effect'. At the moment someone who receives any form of benefit begins to lose the unemployment-related benefit as they start to work. They will then get tax credit benefits as they start to work. However, it is very difficult to get these to work together and at the moment people are in a position where they can work an extra ten hours a week and end up worse off as a result.

This is clearly highly demotivating, especially since benefit sanctions are now forcing people to work longer for less pay. With a Citizen's Income, however, the payment is no longer conditional and is not withdrawn so every single extra hour of paid employment is extra income. It solves the problem of the 'withdrawal effect' completely and ends in one go the problem of the so-called 'benefit trap'.

However, a Citizen's Income at Jobseeker Allowance level is clearly a very modest policy. It is when we realise what can be done with the policy once it is in place that the scope of a citizen's Income becomes clear. It is a policy that is highly redistributive. In future you can increase the value of the Citizen's Income by increasing tax and giving the additional tax revenue straight back to people. Of course, because the citizen's Income is 'flat' (everyone gets the same) but the tax system is progressive (you pay more if you can afford to pay more), each penny tends to redistribute money towards those at the middle and the bottom of the income scale.

There is a simple and elegant way to address all these problems and many more. It is called a Citizen's Income.

There should be a clear commitment to incrementally increasing the Citizens Income rate as unemployment falls, wages increase and tax receipts rise. Small rises in the income tax rate could also bring in significant increases in income which could help with incremental rises in the Citizens Income rate. The combination of an increasing tax base and small increases in tax could allow for a steady rise in the Citizens Income rate to get up to the EU legal requirement of welfare support (40 per cent of median income of EU states).

Finally, even if we end poverty and low pay there are always people who have particular needs, most obviously those with disabilities and people with caring responsibilities. It will always be the case that some people will have some specific additional needs for which they will require support on a means-tested basis. A Citizen's Income will cover the cost of living for people who are unable to work for health reasons and an additional payment would be made for those who have extra costs associated with their impairment or other health related problem.

A Common Weal Scotland is built on security for all of its citizens. We need to create a robust system of social security which provides a solid foundation for people so they can participate in society and the economy on the basis of security and confidence.

Chapter Eight

FINANCIAL SECURITY

We can create a wealthier, fairer nation

Use a full programme of the policies needed to raise
incomes and reduce inequality.

Build a community banking system which is secure and
which customers trust.

Build a sustainable pensions solution.

Regulate finance to make sure it is stable and
no risk to the economy.

Inequality lives everywhere and affects everyone but pretends always to be somewhere else and always to be someone else's problem. Most of us think that inequality is something that impacts on other people. Many of us believe that where we are – what we earn, what we own, how and where we live – is 'normal'. But is it?

The average salary in Scotland is about £25,000. The average salary in Norway is about £45,000. The average salary of the poorest tenth of the Scottish working population is about £6,500. The average salary of the poorest tenth of the population in Norway is just a little below £25,000. But most people in Scotland don't earn the average salary – 60 per cent of people who work in Scotland fail to earn that much. So three out of five Scots earn less than the lowest-paid tenth of Norwegian workers.

Now of course the cost of living in Norway is a bit higher than in Britain. But nothing like twice as high. And taxes in Norway are higher too – but again, nothing like twice as high. What we often fail to recognise is that Britain is a cheap country. The deal is that you are hired and fired on the cheap (which they call 'flexible labour markets') and in return what you get is cheap food and cheap clothes. So in return for low wages we have poor-quality processed foods on heavy discount and poor-quality sweatshop clothing which falls apart.

These low-quality, low-price imports then make our own domestic economy uncompetitive by comparison and this means businesses close, jobs are lost and the very corporations which are paying the low wages and importing the cheap, low-quality processed goods take the value of those jobs and exports them as profit. This just keeps making us poorer and keeps undercutting our own economy.

People think inequality is bad for the poor. It is. But it doesn't stop there. Inequality is bad for almost anyone in work – and it is generally worse still for anyone out of work. Certainly for at least 90 per cent of the population a high-wage, more equal society would make them personally and individually more wealthy and more economically secure. There is an easy way to tell if that's you – you'll be earning less than £45,000 (personally, not including any other household income). And even for those earning a little over that amount, a more equal society would not make you materially worse off as rising wages overall would make almost everyone wealthier.

So if we want to have a wealthier population then there are two straightforward targets: create a high-wage economy and reduce income and wealth inequality.

We have already looked in some depth about how to do this. We need to create an economy that favours high-pay, high-skill, productive enterprises and which encourages all businesses to up-skill their job roles and their workforce. We need a system of industrial democracy that balances the power of corporate employers (who will seek to extract the most value from an enterprise in profit) with more powerful workers (who will seek to extract a larger value from an enterprise in wages). We need a living wage that makes work pay and employment rights that emphasise security of income. We need a social security system that gives people a strong and secure foundation from which they can either seek decent-quality work or to start their own enterprise. We should put in place a Citizen's Income that helps to redistribute wealth.

We should also 'deconsumerise' to reduce the amount of national wealth that is exported by retail multinationals (see below). We should recognise that low-wages/cheap-prices is a bad deal and that high-wages/ real-prices is much better for us. We already tax income progressively and we must do the same with wealth so that wealth held in assets is also taxed fairly.

We need a strong public sector that creates good, well-paid jobs and distributes resources more evenly. We need strong local economies that retain more of the economic value of trade in local communities. We need a proper housing policy to get house prices under control that prevents house prices transferring wealth from households to landlords and financial services. And we need to invest properly in our society so that the elements which grow our shared wealth are themselves grown and supported.

All of this will help Scotland to drag itself up from near the bottom of the league table for inequality and start to produce a nation that shares its wealth fairly through wages and by preventing exploitation of citizens. Even Me-First politicians accept that inequality is bad for society but they usually go on to give the impression that tackling it is beyond the wit of humankind. What they really mean is that it's beyond the narrow limits of their politics. The means of reducing inequality are well known and in fact recently even the International Monetary Fund (which is one of the big institutions of global Me-First politics) has accepted that tackling inequality is necessary to improve economic performance.

So almost everyone becomes wealthier in a more equal society and almost everyone becomes wealthier again as we move to a high-wage economy. But this wealth is the wealth of economic security, not the wealth of greed and waste. The kind of wealth that is created through productivity and equality is by definition not the grotesque wealth promoted by the celebrity lifestyle. It is not the imaginary promise of unlimited riches which Me-First economics promises everyone but delivers for almost no-one. It is the wealth to know that you can live a good, fulfilling, rewarding life for you and your family – and that you can pay the bills at the end of the month.

Me-First economics places a race for income at the heart of its philosophy – higher income is taken to be a proxy for everything that is good in life. Only by wanting more and more can these good things ever be realised. And of course they never are.

John Ruskin wrote "there is no wealth but life". This is the wealth that citizens say they want and it is the wealth that a Common Weal Scotland would deliver. It is wealth that lets you live the life you want without fear or anxiety. Seeking economic security is not lacking in ambition; it is the greatest ambition of all for a society. That all citizens can have the income to live good lives is a wealth beyond anything that Me-First economics offers.

A society that creates and spreads wealth in a way that builds economic security must be underpinned by financial security. That means we need secure, high-quality banking and strong, safe pensions. We need to take the 'casino' element out of our financial system and replace it with safe, reliable – boring – financial security.

The lesson for banking in this country could not be clearer; we need a banking system that is built on trust from customers which comes from banks which care about their customers. It must be a safe banking sector in which your savings are secure and which supports you when you need support – perhaps to get a mortgage to buy a house or to get a loan to start a business. And we must never get into the position again where a corrupt banking system threatens to bring down not only all of our personal finances but the whole economy along with it.

Achieving this is straightforward. We need small, responsive banks that are rooted in their community and which pose no systemic threat to the economy. Once again, this is a model which is normal in western European countries where community and mutually-owned banking is often the dominant model of banking for households. In fact, in both Germany and Japan a large majority of the banking market is local or regional banks and this sector makes up a third of the banking sector in the US.

The balance sheets of the big banks (all their debts and assets) contain an enormous amount of risk – they are still unstable and vulnerable to economic shock. This is a problem made much worse because they remain far too large and each of them individually remains a threat to the entire economy if anything happens to their liquidity (the amount of cash they actually hold). Any system of retail banking (providing current accounts, mortgages and loans to households and small businesses) which is based on these existing banks will be unstable and will require the public to underwrite that instability. Banking is built on confidence but the existing banks give no reason for customers to feel confident and so they need a 'guarantee scheme' funded by taxpayers to reassure customers (and other lenders) that if the bank collapses, the public will pick up the pieces. This is called 'lender of last resort'.

But a Common Weal Scotland cannot be based on an unstable banking system which no-one trusts and which can function only if it is glued together with unlimited guarantees of money from the pockets of the public. We have already seen that the big banks have failed to provide sources of patient funding for large-scale national investment. Those big investment projects (in both the public and private sectors) should be supported by a National Investment Bank (see above).

Then we need to offer customers a secure, stable, trustworthy and reliable retail banking service – and the overall system that these banking services

So almost everyone becomes wealthier in a more equal society and almost everyone becomes wealthier again as we move to a high-wage economy. But this wealth is the wealth of economic security, not the wealth of greed and waste.

make up must not pose unacceptable systemic risk. As we have seen, the existing banking sector does not offer that. It will therefore be necessary to offer customers a better alternative.

That alternative will be boring and safe. It will offer normal, high-quality current account services for households and individuals where you can keep your money, set up direct debits to pay your bills, get money out from cashline machines, pay for things using debit and credit cards and everything else you'd expect from a bank. It would also offer a normal loan service for arranging bank loans for customers when they need them. And it would provide secure mortgages to home-buyers. In fact, it would do all the things that we expect from our bank – except it would be local and locally managed so you will have a bank manager and a staff in the bank who are solely responsible for your account. And it will be the same manager and same staff you deal with next time too.

But perhaps above all these banks will be non-profit generating. They will operate on mutual principles so everyone who keeps money in the bank is a part owner and all profits are put back into the business. There would be no incentive for bankers to make a profit at the expense of their customers and every incentive for them to keep long-term trusting relationships with their customers. It was the hunt for profit at any cost that brought down the UK banking system. It must not be allowed to happen again.

The system will be created with two overlapping kinds of provision. First of all we should replicate the effective German system. Here 43 per cent of the banking market is made up of local and regional publicly-owned banks. Each of the existing local authorities would set up local/regional banks designed to provide precisely the locally-focused, locally-managed, safe and secure banking that people want and need. There would be many branches across the local authority area and indeed it would be possible to provide banking facilities for smaller communities from existing local authority premises.

In addition to this sector the development of smaller mutual banks and credit unions will be supported. These can provide a similar but different kind of service for their members and can be tailored to specific needs. For example, in poorer communities it may be credit unions that provide the kind of micro-finance loans which are currently delivered expensively by pay day loan companies (these companies that target the already limited wealth of the poor to make giant private profits for their owners should no longer exist in a Common Weal Scotland).

All of these banks would then be linked to each other through an association and service provider company that is owned jointly by the independent local banks. This association and shared company will ensure easy interaction between these different banks so where there are efficiencies of scale (benefits from doing things collectively) there is a vehicle for doing that. It would also set strict regulation and restrictions on community banks, so that, for example, community banks could not expand beyond a permitted geographical boundary to prevent the tendency towards monopolisation in banking. Clear societal goals would have to be strictly adhered to so, for example, community banks couldn't fund local projects that are damaging to the local environment.

Once a system of community banking is in place that offers supportive and secure banking services, a government education effort will be initiated to explain to domestic customers the benefits of moving their finance to these community banks. Credit unions and smaller mutual banks and building societies, subject to their own set of strict rules and regulations, will pick up other customer needs.

For most local businesses the community banking system will also meet their needs. They will be able to get business account services and access to borrowing in an environment where they can develop long-term relationships with their bank. It is also possible that these banks may provide some of the sources of finance for local investment in infrastructure – although large-scale, riskier lending must be discouraged.

The community banking sector will be entirely independent and run locally according to local need. It will not be centrally managed and nor will it have centrally-set targets (although within the strict regulations of the sector). However, there should be an open flow of information between the banks and the National Investment Bank to enable an overview to be taken of both the levels of investment being made across the country and to identify any emerging systemic risk resulting from the individual actions of a lot of different banks. The central bank would also issue direct guidance to banks on the amount of credit they can issue so as to prevent risky credit bubbles.

Once this banking system is in place it should be made clear that it is the public sector's responsibility to ensure the value of savings and to ensure that suitable amounts of credit are available in the wider economy. It is not the public sector's job to guarantee the business of any individual bank or financial service company. A Scottish central bank (if we have one) or the National Investment Bank (if we don't) should guarantee individual savings are secure and provide loans if banks don't but it should not offer a blanket lender of last resort facility to all banks in all circumstances. Banks which have made commercial decisions, that have acted speculatively, that have become 'too big to fail' and so on can't possibly imagine that the general public will underwrite their behaviour indefinitely. Private-sector banks are free to take risks – as long as the risk is to the individual bank or enterprise and not the economy as a whole.

To ensure this, we therefore have to introduce regulation on private-sector banks so that the wider public are protected from their speculative activities by a firewall. The first measure is to re-introduce a new form of the 'Glass-Steagal' act, a legal separation between investment and commercial banking. This means risky investment decisions are separated from the bank accounts of ordinary customers. This may require Government to have the legislative power to break up big-banks themselves that are measured as a threat to the wider economy and the financial system as a whole because of their size.

Secondly, we need to introduce credit controls which specifically limit asset-based credit creation and speculation so as to avoid asset-based inflation, especially in the housing market, and discourage excessive risk-taking in the financial markets. Put simply, banks can't just create new money to push up prices and increase profits. To do this a higher reserve requirement for assets would be set. By setting the rate at a higher level than for, say, deposit liabilities means that the cost of short-term loans and risky investments is raised relative to long-term loans. This can encourage more socially useful, productive financial investment.

One public asset that has been subject to risky speculation by the trustees of the UK's occupational pension schemes is private pensions. Trustees are responsible for the investment policies of pension funds and they have chosen to hand over pension money to the financial markets to speculate with. Providing security for those who have retired from work will be more difficult because of the poor starting position of the UK on pensions, but social security means work pays, people out of work are protected and those who have retired can live comfortably. So pensions matter.

There are three pillars of the UK pensions industry – the state pension (paid to everyone), the occupational pension (a fund paid into by employees collectively) and private pensions (sold to an individual by a financial services company). All face major problems in the UK. The British state pension is now the lowest in the developed world. The occupational pension schemes are in real trouble with almost all now abandoning guarantees of what they will pay out. The private pension industry in the UK is a disgrace of dreadful regulation and exploitation in which companies have been taking one pound of every three saved by people for their pensions for 'administration'. The outcome is that in the UK there is an assumption that old age will become an increasingly difficult time for people and that accepting a lower standard of living and later and later retirement is the only option.

There is a problem with pensions. From the 1980s until the financial crash, pension schemes had promised to deliver generous pensions from modest contributions based on high rates of return on investment (sometimes assuming eight per cent returns and more every year). These pension funds sought out high-return investment options to meet those targets – but the high-return options turned out to be high-risk options which were unsustainable. This pressure to make high-risk investments on a continuous basis played a large part in creating the financial crisis. In any case, these investments were generally based, at least in part, on financial returns that were illusory. We have to accept that in pensions, like so much else, the promise of Me-First economics (that you can have good pensions on low contributions because of financial speculation) was never true. We need to plan into the future on the basis of a more modest expectation of what investment markets can do for pensions.

We need to take a much firmer regulatory position on the pensions and asset management industry to require it to be much more honest about likely returns and to stop the rampant profiteering from management charges which have stolen so much of the value of people's pensions. If pensions and asset managers were regulated in this way it would increase the value of pensions for the sum invested by the individual, but at the same time it would be much clearer that these are comparatively expensive ways to provide for retirement.

So secondly, we need to repair the occupational pensions industry. Poor management of pension funds (including 'contribution holidays' where money was skimmed off in the good times) and declining rates of return on investment mean that we need to create bigger, better managed options. During an initial transition period of perhaps a decade or so, Scotland should seek to create a national occupational pension fund which anyone would have a right to pay in to and which employers would also be required to contribute. The first phase of forming this fund would involve the consolidation of funded public sector pension funds into one large fund. This can be done without affecting the existing pension rights of the members of these schemes. Thereafter, this fund would be expanded to take in transfers from defined contribution pension funds and new entrants on terms that make clear what realistically they can expect to receive in their pension upon retirement. The aim is to level up as much as possible to the standard of pension provision in public sector schemes, which, whilst not as 'generous' as many commentators allege, do provide a firm link between earnings and pension. The projected earnings-related pensions would be based on a careful calculation of the level of contributions being paid into the fund and the level of benefits that this income, together with investment returns, can support. We should aim to provide earnings-related pensions where a certain level of pension can be guaranteed rather than the 'defined contribution' model where the pension is uncertain and all the pensioner bears all the risk.

This pension fund should then invest on an entirely different basis. At the moment pension funds invest heavily in securities markets. These are various forms of financial speculation which deliver returns on investment which – like all speculation – are based on spurious and volatile market conditions. This is the casino end of finance where everything is always brilliant – until it

We need small, responsive banks which are rooted in their community and which pose no systemic threat to the economy. Once again, this is a model which is normal in European countries where community and mutually-owned banking is often the dominant model of banking for households.

isn't. Instead pension funds should accept lower rates of returns on investment than speculation at its peak but which are solid, real-world investments in the real economy which over the lifetime of the investment are stable and guaranteed. This means investing in the real economy.

Pension funds can be used as a major source of capitalisation of a National Investment Bank. This is a win-win model where pension wealth (which after all is the wealth of citizens) is invested in the economy and actively benefits citizens. Unlike investing in speculative markets investing in the real economy not only provides returns but actually grows the economy so even greater returns to the public good are achieved over time.

But again, we need to be realistic about the rate of return involved. While we must aim to provide defined benefit pensions it is inevitable that there must be a compromise struck between aspiration and affordability. The level of guaranteed pensions must be set in accordance with realistic rates of contributions and realistic levels of expected investment returns. Prosperity in retirement, like all prosperity, depends on real wealth creation in the economy. But this does not mean that we need simply to accept that all the risk is borne by the person saving for a pension. We must make sure that risk is shared across the whole of society, including employers, through a national occupational pension scheme, and via the retired person's Citizen's Income (which would replace the state pension).

We should move from the state pension being a 'safety net' for the poorest pensioners and a 'top up' for others, to a more substantial guaranteed pension becoming a fundamental part of the economic security of most citizens upon retirement. This of course fits well with a citizen's Income model and it is this which should form the basis for income in retirement with occupational and private pension schemes more likely to offer a substantial 'top up' rather than the other way round.

In all of this, financial regulation must be predicated on an entirely different premise than it is currently. At the moment, regulation is structured around the needs of hedge funds, derivatives and general financial speculation, which is the shaky foundation on which the financial services sector builds its wealth. This doesn't make any sense; finance is too central to the economy to be regulated on the basis of profit maximisation. Rather we must regulate financial services on the basis of stability and security. Far from this choking off the financial services sector in Scotland it offers it an opportunity to develop specialism in secure investment. Edinburgh could become a global centre of 'boring banking', the place where people come to invest safely and securely. Banking innovation need not mean constantly increasing recklessness but, like industry, can be a process of smart specialisation. Given the world's financial position, secure and safe might well be just such a specialisation.

A Common Weal Scotland is built on creating economic security for citizens that enables them to live a good life free from financial fears and anxieties.

Chapter 9

HUMAN SECURITY

If we take real threats seriously we can protect our
nation and our people

Have a modest system of territorial defence.

Invest in human security and environmental protection.

Create a policing and criminal justice system that reduces crime in the long term.

Break organised crime's hold on vulnerable communities.

Tackle violence against women by taking measures to address gender inequalities.

Tackle head-on the causes of public health problems that threaten citizens.

We have seen how to create economic and social security. We should then think about the other aspects of security which are important to our lives – crime-free communities, public health, natural disasters, territorial protection. This is known as human security. Traditional models of defence have been based on the concept of protecting state boundaries and securing access to resources. There is still a manufactured 'truth' that the main purpose is preventing attack from opposing armed forces or protecting overseas interests. The contemporary reality, however, is that an attack on state boundaries by an invading army is not considered even a moderate risk.

The current risks to Scotland arise principally from our use as military real estate. In particular we are the base for the UK's nuclear arsenal with 180 nuclear bombs housed 25 miles from Glasgow and we have the regular transportation of warheads through our towns and cities en route from the south. A refocusing of the concept of defence policy to human security policy is long overdue and will encourage a proper evaluation of priorities. Does it make more of a contribution to our security to spend money on flood defence, the Serious Organised Crime Unit, Women's Aid, Violence Reduction Units, prevention of environmental pollution and global warming or to spend it on more military hardware? It also raises questions of what causes conflicts and demands for international intervention. So often it is poverty, resource scarcity, corporate exploitation and environmental degradation that have been the triggers for wars. Tackling the causes including the behaviour of rich states and corporations, makes more sense than financing military intervention.

Scotland should simply stop playing the military-defence industry game. Scotland is a threat to others because of our nuclear role and our involvement with the UK's wars. Scotland just should not be a threat to anyone. We do not need to be involved in aggressive expeditionary military action of the kind that has dominated UK policy. Making a contribution where appropriate to UN peacekeeping activities should be our only military external role. Even looking at small European countries, we can see many examples of valuable contributions to peacemaking and disarmament. Scotland could establish an International Peacemaking Academy with the aim of becoming a centre of excellence in training for diplomacy, mediation, non-violent action, cultural awareness, reintegration of militias and the study of causal factors in conflict.

Scotland is arguably in the single most geostrategically stable region in the world. No matter what direction you draw a line in from Scotland, the first landfall is another developed nation and ally. We are surrounded by the most stable and developed countries in the world. There is not a single credible territorial threat to Scotland from any state anywhere in the world. An invasion of Scotland by a hostile force is as close to a zero-chance event as there is in global politics.

The same is true of terrorism; while the threat of terrorism is never zero, the international terrorist threat is lower in Scotland than in the vast majority of EU nations, not least as a result of our geographical position. Indeed, most of the terrorist threat to Scotland arises from the fact that Scotland – as a part of the UK – is complicit in the UK's military interventions and its support for questionable governments in the Middle East and beyond.

So Scotland should not base its future on preparing a defence against a threat that will not arise. It should certainly not build its future based on unwanted (and illegal) military interventions in other countries. We should not be interested in 'projecting power'. Where we should focus defence is on the area the UK has arguably neglected – the 'home front'. We should shape our defence focus by prioritising – first and foremost – the security of its land, sea and people.

Scotland is a maritime nation whose sea area is more than five times larger than its land area. It has over 11,000 km of highly indented coastline – amounting to approximately 61 per cent of the total UK coastline – and over

800 islands. If there is a Scottish Defence Force (SDF) it should be tasked and equipped primarily to patrol and defend Scotland's sizeable coastline, sea and airspace. This would require a proficient Scottish Navy and Air Force, incorporating a Coastguard Service and working closely with a dedicated Scottish Customs Agency.

While Scotland's physical structure and location afford great opportunities, it also carries some risks – Scotland's close proximity to continental Europe and Ireland has resulted in a host of smuggling activities around and through Scotland. Those activities have seen the transportation of – amongst other things – contraband cigarettes and alcohol, people trafficked for labour and the sex industry, and weapons arriving in or passing through Scotland, with predictable accompanying damage to government revenues and to human wellbeing. This is our challenge – not imaginary invasions.

It should not be forgotten that Scotland's economic interests in its surrounding seas are certain to increase in the coming decades, perhaps most notably across the various energy fields. Ecological concerns may also rise as the opening up of the Northern Sea Route – facilitated by the rapid melting of key areas of Arctic sea ice – sees greater volumes of shipping along Scotland's western and eastern seaboards. A lack of understanding of, and careless engagement with these developments could compromise the ecological integrity of the seas, which surround Scotland, damaging Scotland's fisheries industry, Scottish tourism, and the wider wellbeing of Scotland's people and wildlife.

It is these issues that should define how an independent Scotland thinks about, and prioritises, its security and defence. The main strength of an SDF should reside in its aerial and maritime capability, with reconnaissance aircraft and an ocean-going fleet which are capable of undertaking maritime patrol and surveillance, customs enforcement, search and rescue operations, and fisheries protection duties.

The legacy of the UK Government's 'defence' approach in Scotland should be dealt with in a speedy fashion. The Trident nuclear submarines and weapons system should be dismantled and removed from Faslane as soon as is safe and sensible to do so.

The SDF could operate internationally in co-ordination with UN mandated operations. With a modest but highly-trained army, an independent Scotland might well seek to forge a reputation for proficiency in fields such as peacekeeping and humanitarian operations. The ways in which Scottish forces could be used should be heavily restrained by dedicated articles in a constitution. Given this approach, it's not apparent what utility entry into broader military alliances, like NATO, would serve Scotland in its own defence or overseas operations.

A sensible and proportionate response to Scotland's territorial defensive needs should be matched with a sensible and proportionate response to the more pressing human security threats Scotland faces. Human security is based on the idea that national security is not about the interests of the state itself but of its citizens. This is why a national security approach may invest heavily in military hardware that suits the interests of some of the nations elite but does nothing for citizens, whereas a human security approach would focus on for example investment in flood mitigation and reducing pollution that really harm the lives of real people.

The most important aspects of human security relate to the sustainable management of the environment. Of course, Scotland must not only play its part in reducing the production of CO_2 which causes climate change but seek to lead the world on environmentally sustainable development. We already have some of the most ambitious targets set by any nation and we need to invest and to act to achieve them. Scotland is one of the world's richest countries in terms of wind, wave, tide and rain-fed hydro energy. To meet our potential we need investment in renewable energy, investment in housing to improve thermal performance, shifting to a hydrogen economy (where more is powered by clean hydrogen and less by dirty carbon), reducing energy usage through changed work patterns, land use planning, investment in low-emission and zero-carbon transport and a range of other actions already discussed above.

We then have to act to address the impacts of environmental degradation in Scotland. We have already looked at land use, the need to mitigate intensive farming, to have more tree belt and better management of land. This will protect us from a number of human security threats. For example, regular breaks between land which is intensively farmed where trees and shrubs are protected greatly helps absorb run-off from heavy rain to reduce flooding. Better land management will protect the threats to top soil quality and quantity which in turn threaten our ability to be 'food sovereign' (be capable of ensuring secure food supplies for all citizens, even in the event of a global crisis).

We have also already looked at how investment in housing and heating technologies (including biomass, geothermal and solar) can rapidly reduce our reliance on imported energy sources which make us vulnerable to severe energy shortages in the event of global crisis.

In taking this approach, we can reconfigure our approach to public investment in preparing for threats to our national wellbeing that reflect not the interests of arms dealers but of citizens. We would invest not just in military hardware, which plays little role in making us safer, but also in environmental management which does.

We then need to ensure that people are secure in their communities. This means that we need an approach to policing and criminal justice that emphasises long-term community security.

To achieve this we need to recognise that inequalities and structural injustice are closely connected with victimisation, offending and fear of crime. When we recognise that many of the problems of crime affect communities which suffer from deprivation and poverty it becomes clear that we have to balance the need for formal justice and security with positive approaches which promote hope, conflict resolution and reconciliation and social justice. An endless cycle of simply seeking to punish offenders will, on its own, not resolve the social harm that crime causes.

The criminal justice process should not prioritise efficiency and financial goals over the need to treat both accused and complainants with fairness, respect and to be supported as appropriate. The potential to develop restorative solutions, conflict resolution, peacemaking and reconciliation in parallel with, or as an alternative to, criminal justice responses should be recognised as a realistic and hopeful means of addressing the needs of both accused and complainants and their families and communities affected by crime.

So while some have argued that there are operational and efficiency advantages to a merged Police Scotland, it is essential to be clear that the primary policing goal of improving safety and wellbeing will only be achieved in a sustainable way when accessibility and engagement with local communities is prioritised and effective accountability enhanced and protected.

Where a national approach is needed is to tackle organised crime and corruption. This is a very important issue in creating a Common Weal Scotland – organised crime has a corrupting effect on many aspects of social and community life if it isn't dealt with rigorously. As well as a policing focus

This is why a national security approach may invest heavily in military hardware that suits the interests of some of the nations elite but does nothing for citizens, whereas a human security approach would focus on for example investment in flood mitigation and reducing pollution that really harm the lives of real people.

on targeting organised crime there must be a national focus on much more punitive financial penalties upon those involved and the professionals who aid them. Organised crime grows when it is profitable and shrinks when it isn't so we need to target the profits of crime – and addressing criminal issues such as drugs policy where prohibition approaches have increased the profitability of organised crime.

Scotland should be a country that takes its legal and international obligations seriously as they relate to children and young people in conflict with the law. The Kilbrandon philosophy, which emphasised 'needs' and 'deeds' as two sides of the same coin remains hugely relevant some fifty years after it was originally outlined. A fundamental rethinking of Scotland's response to children in trouble should address issues such as an age of criminal responsibility which remains one of the lowest in Europe at eight years, with the age of criminal prosecution set at 12 years old, and that at 16, a young person is at risk of being dealt with in the adult court and penal system.

Scotland shares the dubious distinction, along with England and Wales, of having one of the highest imprisonment rates in western Europe. Most prisoners and other people with convictions subject to orders, come from backgrounds of disadvantage. Yet 'justice' continues to be equated with punitive sanctions such as imprisonment. The significant costs of these sanctions may be better re-invested in vulnerable communities to prevent the offending in the first place. Sanctions that are imposed should aim to reduce re-offending but do so in ways that promote the longer term (re)integration of citizens who have convictions, with family, friends and wider society.

Security of all citizens also means creating a Scotland that does not tolerate gender-based violence, exploitation, or abuse. Violence against women is part of wider gender inequalities that remain stubbornly part of our lives. Women in Scotland earn less than men, depend more on the shrinking pot of welfare benefits, and are more likely than men to have insecure, low-paid work. The pay gap in Scotland widened last year, signifying a swathe of households in which single mothers go without food so that their children can be fed and women leave the labour market because the cost of childcare has become greater than their wage.

Domestic abuse is more likely to be found in households with a wider gap between male and female earnings. Women who have experienced domestic abuse, when asked which interventions would be most effective and helpful list childcare, housing, income support and education and skills above refuges. Economic inequality restricts choices, reduces access to justice, and makes it impossible to 'just leave' – whether what is being left is an exploitative workplace or a violent home.

However expressed, violence against women it is a Me-First resource for exercising power, and is a consequence but also a cause of wider gender inequality. It reproduces the conditions that sustain that inequality. So do the everyday, routine, mundane misogynist 'banter' and the colonisation of our lives by pornographic images. Addressing violence against women is not simply about counting up incidents or providing good services for victims and survivors but about recognising the social behaviours and expectations that cause it.

To tackle everything from women's greater rates of poverty to their political underrepresentation we must act. A constitutional right to equality would be one place to start. The approaches which can change this are the 'mainstreaming' of gender, of using laws, policies, services, and budgets to distribute power and resources more equitably between women and men, the use of gender budget analysis as a tool to assess the impact of spending decisions on women and men and boys and girls. Citizen's Income, social security, universal childcare, shorter working week, flexible contracts, quotas to create critical mass in industrial sectors and the use of an industrial policy will help the workplace situation of women.

A final aspect of our collective security is that we have a public health system that reduces the threat of ill health that every one of us faces. Health is one of the most valued assets that individuals and populations can have – if you ask people what security and wellbeing involves for them they will put their health high on the list. Health has different dimensions – positive (feeling good, being able to be physically active), negative (illness, premature death), physical and mental. Many of the measures of population health in Scotland have improved markedly over the last 150 years. Life expectancy has increased from around 40 years to over 75 years, infant mortality has reduced radically and many of the fears of falling ill and becoming destitute have reduced following the introduction of the National Health Service in 1948.

Despite these many successes, health in Scotland has not improved as quickly as in other nations. Life expectancy here has increased more slowly than in other developed countries, particularly since the 1950s, leaving us with the lowest life expectancy in western and central Europe. We do not have good measures of positive wellbeing for Scotland that go back that far, but there has been little improvement in the past 10 years and the international evidence suggests that most high income countries have seen little or no change for decades.

Even more damning than the average health record for the Scottish population is the record on health inequalities. Health inequalities are the systematic and unfair differences in health outcomes seen across social groups, and they are wider here than in the rest of western and central Europe. Within Scotland there is an 11 year gap in healthy life expectancy between the most and least deprived tenths of the population for men, and a 14 year gap for women. Furthermore, premature mortality rates (when people die before 75 years) were more than three times higher in the most deprived groups compared to the least deprived groups. Across Glasgow, there are vast differences in life expectancy between the most affluent areas and the poorest areas. For example, there is a difference in life expectancy of almost 14 years for men and over eight years for women between Jordanhill in the leafy West End and Bridgeton in the east of the city.

Inequalities in health have grown substantially during the last 30 years, driven largely by increases in alcohol and drug-related deaths, suicide and violence – all of which affected young adults predominantly – alongside continuing inequalities in heart disease, strokes and cancer which, although the rates of mortality were improving, still exhibited huge inequalities. A further phenomenon has also been noted over the last 30 to 40 years – the emergence of an 'excess mortality' in Scotland compared to England and Wales, over and above that which could be explained by higher levels of poverty and deprivation (the so-called 'Scottish Effect'). This has emerged over the same time period as the increase in health inequalities and is the subject of a large ongoing programme of research. It's not just about lifestyle or quality of healthcare.

What does the evidence tell us would improve health and reduce health inequalities? The health of any population is determined by the context in which people live. This includes influences from the global environmental scale, through international and national politics and the social and economic conditions experienced, to the social and family networks people are supported by, to the behaviours people adopt and genetics they were born with. These influences occur from before birth and throughout life. You could say 'it all matters' when considering the influences on health.

Fortunately, there is substantial evidence now available from decades of research about the types of politics, policies, interventions and contexts that can support a healthy and equitable society. These include moves such as living income, adequate social security, redistributive policies, labour market interventions, participatory democracy, better housing, stronger community control, less pollution, healthier food, better conditions at work and more. Which is to say that the real steps towards better public health come from precisely the sorts of economic and social change that would be a Common Weal Scotland.

Scotland, particularly in view of the recent moves towards privatisation and commodification of healthcare provision in England, has one of the most efficient and effective healthcare services in the world. It achieves universal healthcare provision, free at the point of need, commanding huge public support and in an affordable and sustainable way. However, there are aspects that should be improved and there are substantial challenges to the continuation of services in the future.

Demographic change and the ageing of the population are likely to increase demand for health and social services into the future. The cost of the service is therefore going to increase and there will be a requirement to retain efficiency in the system. Although unpopular at times, the work of bodies such as the Scottish Medicines Consortium will become more important in ensuring that the pharmaceutical industry does not continue to present industry-sponsored studies as evidence of effectiveness (and often using industry-sponsored patient groups to generate pressure on politicians to use the NHS as a cash cow for pharmaceutical companies). Reducing healthcare demand through effective public policy as described above, allied with evidence-based healthcare innovation governed by high quality public research, will therefore be important for the future. The creation of a publicly owned pharmaceutical industry for Scotland would be an important component of a sustainable healthcare system for the future.

There are several aspects of how the NHS was created which have left unresolved issues. GP services are not provided in proportion to need (with middle class areas commanding more health expenditure) and as independent contractors can have conflicting priorities between the need to generate profits and the need to provide services. However, the situation is much more critical with dentistry and opticians, where full incorporation into the NHS is essential. The lack of a clear democratic oversight mechanism for the NHS has been relatively successful in avoiding overt politicisation of the service and has allowed the integrity of the national service to be maintained. However, the local implementation of the service could be integrated into the democratic structures of local government and thereby generate a much more accountable system. Expanding the role of patients in governing the operation of GP projects should also be explored. Social care services should become fully funded and universal, but also provided as part of an integrated NHS and social care system. Changing the accountability of the NHS towards local authorities would assist this process.

A Common Weal Scotland is built on prioritising the security of its citizens first.

Chapter Ten

DESIGN FOR LIFE

We can design a Scotland that makes life good

Embrace design as a blueprint for our future.

Plan our towns and cities for human use.

Provide great facilities and amenities locally.

Reverse the relentless drive to push people to
constantly consume.

Put participating, learning, making and doing at the heart
of our lives.

Invest in arts and creativity for all.

Help our citizens discover their country and its cultures.

Make schools a place where we make great citizens.

No wealth but life – how did we forget this in Me-First Britain? Why did we put everything – profit, efficiency, competitiveness, growth, greed – ahead of life in our political priorities? The language of modern British politics is meant to sound benign. But words do not mean what they seem to mean. 'Reform' actually means 'cut' or 'end'. 'Flexibility' really means 'exploit'. 'Prudence' actually means 'don't invest'. And 'efficient'? That means whatever you want it to mean – usually 'cut'. All really mean 'keep wages low for the masses, taxes low for the rich, profits high for the corporations and accept the decline in public service and public amenities that this will cause'.

But what has any of this got to do with our lives? Remember what our hopes are; somewhere nice to live, financial security, time with family, good services, strong community, a sense of self respect. What words are there in British politics to describe these hopes? 'Rewarding hard working families'? Well the reward they want is time with each other and financial security – and they're certainly not getting that.

Britain is designed for profit maximisation. It is a nation that has become built on the principle of take as much out as you can while putting as little in as you can and all in the shortest possible time. It describes our politics, it describes our economy, it describes our leisure time – it even describes our television talent shows, our National Lottery, our 'buy a team' approach to sport. Skill and collective endeavour are from the 'olden days'; what we are really supposed to admire are luck and wealth.

Scotland's mission must be to design for life. Where we have two choices we must take the one that makes life better for people, not the one that makes profit bigger for corporations. Everything until this point has been an attempt to explain how we create a social and economic structure for Scotland that is designed for life or designed to create a foundation for life. But work isn't life. Budgeting isn't life. Building isn't life. All these things influence our lives but they do not define our lives.

Life is about how we experience being alive. Each of us must make our own minds up about what experience of being alive is important to us. It will not be the same answer for any two of us. Some of us love the exhaustion of trying to meet a challenge. Some of us love the stillness of tranquillity and reflection. Some of us are driven by a moral belief in something we must do. Some of us are driven by a need to express ourselves. Some of us find our greatest happiness in the garden, some of us find our greatest happiness among our friends.

Stop and ask yourself; what have you done of which you are most proud? What have you done that made you happy? What is your biggest contribution to your community? What has felt important to your life? When you're gone, what is the most significant thing you'll have left behind? Whose life did you touch and make better? What will you regret if you don't try it? What do you still hope to achieve?

This will tell you what matters to you, what counts. Now ask yourself; has my government made what matters to me easier or harder to achieve? Is the society and the economy we have helping me to realise the life that I want to live? What are the barriers to what I want to do and how I want to be? Where did those barriers come from? Why are they allowed to persist?

We accept too easily the existence of conditions that stop us from living – long working hours, low pay, insecurity and anxiety, poor quality housing and local facilities, debt-fuelled consumption, declining environment. We really shouldn't. We really can design a society that gives us the best chance of a good life.

Design and innovation are at the forefront of our hopes for the future. A new generation of designers of all sorts is challenging the old order. Do products have to be mass-manufactured in sweatshops? Do the goods in our house have to harm the environment in which we live? Must things be designed to wear out, be replaced, wear out, be replaced? Can't our communities be planned with good spaces to play in? Is the way we access our public services as intuitive as it can be? Just because we did things like this yesterday is that the best way to do them today?

Scotland is very lucky – we have genuinely world-class universities and art schools that produce generations of highly-skilled graduates who are driven by an ethos of design and innovation. We have an excellent college sector training people in the practices of design and innovation. There are networks of young designers and innovative manufacturing enterprises and improving facilities for micro-engineering and prototyping. All of this is a wonderful resource for Scotland's future.

So how are we using this resource? Have we created an economy and a public sector in which the market for the best of these young design-driven professionals is fierce as both business and public services see their future lying in innovation? No. We have low rates of innovation right across the economy and the public sector and a profit-maximising attitude to economic development that favours fast return not patient development. We import yesterday's ideas from China; we should be exporting tomorrow's ideas from Scotland.

A national 'design for life' policy would force us to look at how we use our public space and how we use our public services to see how we make those services and those spaces what we want them to be.

Our approaches to where and how we live are failing us. Towns and cities are designed on the basis of profit. Land is treated as a speculative asset. We clear or make land available for development. At this point the land becomes highly speculatively valuable and is bought by property development companies. Their only interest is then to create the maximum profit possible from developing that land. This means that they produce commercial medium-density housing with low build standards and poor planning and amenities. Medium-density housing is neither genuinely set in spacious surroundings nor properly planned to make the best use of space. Small, detached houses are crammed together with little private space and very little shared space. They are seldom built to last. The aim of this housing is not to provide the best environment for families but to extract the maximum possible value from the land they are built on.

There is no wealth but life – how did we forget this in Me-First Britain?

Once they are built and sold the developer has extracted all the value from the land and will move on to look for the next piece of land to extract the value from. What is left behind are poorly-planned communities in housing which is cheaply built and so deteriorates quickly. The profit is taken out of the land and so its value drops. Comparatively quickly these new-build developments become declining housing estates. Eventually they may be designated as areas for development, will be cleared and the whole process starts again.

In city centres the process is even more damaging. Here land is largely all developed and so the only way that corporations can extract the value of the land is if it is cleared for development. By definition it will be older, less valuable housing which is cleared and it will be replaced with new-build marketed directly at the wealthy middle classes. Here the process of extracting land value not only creates badly-designed spaces but clears working class families from cities and forces them into peripheral housing estates.

The outcome of 30 years of Me-First, design-for-profit property development has been two-fold. Firstly it has transferred large amounts of wealth from families to corporations and wealthy developers – the price that you are paying for your house is largely the result of decades of intensive trade in land value. Secondly, it has created an urban landscape which is badly designed, bad to live in, unsustainable and poorly constructed. We have entire communities in medium-density housing schemes with no local facilities, no local economy and no social space. In many of these developments access to even basic services like a grocers can only be reached by car. People do not bump into each other in the street on their way to the newsagent. They have no public parks so when the weather is nice each family is crammed into their own postage-stamp garden, not sharing in community life. Children don't have safe space to play. Schools are no longer places you walk to; no-one can jump on a bike and cycle to their work. The rooms that you live in in your house are sized not to allow you the best possible life but to squeeze in the largest possible number of detached houses in a given space.

In Britain we live in the smallest houses in Europe. We lack private space, we lack public space, often we design-out any local economy at all, we take little interest in the space and play needs of children and we build in patterns that are actively harmful to community life and neighbourliness.

This also squanders high-quality assets that we have. Much of this process involves knocking down perfectly viable houses and replacing them with housing which is of a lower build quality. As we have seen, this is because the business opportunity is really in the land, not in the housing. Renovating existing housing creates more and better jobs than knocking houses down and rebuilding them – which means the profits for corporations are lower.

This is reflected in a set of utterly perverse incentives, which seem designed to encourage us to knock down our heritage and move in to rubbish houses far away from the communities we have built our lives in. If you build a new house you do not pay VAT. If you renovate an existing house you pay VAT at 20 per cent. So rather than repairing and improving what are often fundamentally good-quality homes we are instead knocking them down. It is essential that we immediately equalise VAT on new-build and renovation, charging both at a reduced rate of five per cent. This has been shown to promote regeneration, increase the supply of homes by encouraging empty homes back into use at the hearts of their communities, reduce the black economy and increase employment – repair being more labour, and less resource, intensive.

The impact of planning decisions in the business sector simply compound the impacts of planning decisions in the residential sector. Profit maximisation found out-of-town shopping developments very attractive. They build the infrastructure on very cheap land using the cheapest possible construction methods (these are basically sheds in fields) all of which is fuelled by public sector planning decisions. This means that policies, which are supposed to represent the public interest, are used to enable low-investment companies to pitch up outside existing communities and undercut the local economy. It has led to the devastation of local economies, high streets and local communities.

The final nails in the coffin of many communities come from developing public amenities using private finance arrangements with no local control. Finance deals for public infrastructure are driven by identifying profit for the developer and much of this, again, has come from trading the land. It is creating a Scotland where schools are on the outskirts of communities rather than in communities. Hospitals are designed to squeeze as much on the land as possible and not to help people get better. You will likely have lost your local football pitch to a property developer – and instead gained a giant sports centre three towns away.

We need to begin again. As we have seen, what Scotland needs is not an increased supply of the kind of housing which is stripping wealth from families and communities while killing the local area and harming the environment. We need a massive increase in the supply of high-quality, spacious public rented housing which is designed to improve the life of communities. And planning and tax decisions must not be driven by 'economic growth' goals but 'design for life' goals.

The physical environment provides the places and spaces in which we are more-or-less happy, more-or-less creative and more-or-less economically-effective. A proper measure of the 'more', rather than the 'less', is the amount of amenity, or utility, a built environment offers us: the nearby parks, schools and shops, its connectivity via a nice, easy route to work or by good access to its public buildings. How it allows and encourages the ways we creatively interact with each other from park bench to great places of public assembly, and how all relate to nature and sunshine.

First and foremost, we need to regain confidence in the idea of public services and the democratic right for all to have easy access to these services, as well as to complimentary commercial ones, would see them fortified in their existing, town centre locations under the Town Centre first principle, where public transport goes, rather than dispersed out-of-town, where the car owner gets stuck in traffic. The use of new powers (as proposed above) over community democracy and community land ownership would give local communities the powers to access and use its land and buildings together.

Delivering all this would be a radically-revised planning system, which would answer the question 'why does society build?' by putting utility at its heart. Hospitals that use light, fresh air and access to nature to promote healing;. Homes and communities built round sunshine and shared space. Offices focussed on creative working environments. Schools focussed on light, playspace and their location in their communities. Villages, towns and cities focussed on parks, walking and shared space.

Just as the physical environment needs to be designed for life rather than profit, so does our social environment.

Over the last 40 years public policy has supported the endless expansion of hyper-consumerism. When your economy doesn't make things and has a poor productivity record, other ways of making corporate profit must be identified. As we have seen repeatedly, this has been achieved by structuring the economy to enable corporations to extract the maximum wealth from consumers as quickly and as continuously as possible. We structure our city centres primarily for the benefit of the retail industry and in the case of large shopping malls we actually build city centre public space which is run privately for profit where other activities are banned. We not only accept but encourage saturation advertising and we have a very light-touch approach to regulating how advertising impacts on different groups in society (notably children). That regulation has declined with commercial sectors like drink, gambling and payday loans dominating where they used to be strictly controlled as they are harmful activities.

So much of the fabric of modern life is designed to promote consumption, from the banking industry with its cheap debt and easy credit to the marketing partnerships enthusiastically entered into by public sector bodies (a big sporting event in Britain is so heavily branded it looks like a shopping mall with a race going on inside it). But perhaps the final straw was when leading politicians embedded the rhetoric of consumerism into the heart of political debate. It was the political class that started to use 'footfall on the high street' as a fundamental indicator of economic health and developed a patronising narrative of 'the punters don't really care about international issues or the state of the nation, they care about shoes and corporate football and having a drink and going to bingo'.

The impacts of hyper-consumerism are significant. Perhaps prime among them are that it created an economy which strips our income from us but puts very little back into our society. It has been at the heart of the low-pay, unproductive economy. But we must not underestimate the other impacts. Advertising and consumerism is driven by persuading customers that there is something 'wrong' with them which they can 'fix' by spending money. Modern marketing plays on insecurities, amplifies them and seeks to create them where they don't exist. This is all about creating 'status anxiety' – the fear that others will have a low regard for you because your conspicuous consumption (the extent to which the things you own can be seen as evidence that you are 'successful') is insufficient. The anxiety and low

The physical environment provides the places and spaces in which we are more-or-less happy, more-or-less creative and more-or-less economically-effective. A proper measure of the 'more', rather than the 'less', is the amount of amenity, or utility, a built environment offers us: the nearby parks, schools and shops, its connectivity via a nice, easy route to work or by good access to its public buildings.

self esteem that this generates have played an important part in the low levels of mental health and reported happiness in Britain.

There are many other effects – health effects from eating heavily-marketed processed foods and alcohol and because consumption encourages passive behaviours which lead to obesity. The environmental harm of constant consumption is well understood as natural resources are used up faster than they can be replaced and landfill sites everywhere pile up with unwanted junk that does not biodegrade. Over-consumption is also a major driver of inequality since the push to dedicate larger proportions of income to retail expenditure clearly has a deeper impact on those with lower incomes. Finally, consumer-driven debt is undermining the entire financial health of the country and it traps people in a vicious circle in which over-consumption leads to debt that leads to having to work long hours which leads to exhaustion and anxiety which leads to poor diet and stimulates more over-consumption. It traps people in a life that makes them unhappy.

We must re-establish our relationship with the goods we own as part of re-establishing our relationship with our families, friends, communities, society, the outdoor and the environment. We need to re-establish this relationship with goods, so that we value what they mean because of the life they have helped us lead, because of the improvements they have helped us make to our families, community and personal life and because of the lasting enjoyment they have given us. We must re-establish a relationship for consumer goods and those who make them so that they work for us, rather than us working for them.

We need to develop a different materialism, not the materialism of cheap social symbols from the fast fashion we wear or the easily copied brands we buy. Nor the cheap materialism of the poorly made transient goods whose material input is devastatingly expensive for the environment and to those make them and whose material worth as a sustainable source of value in the future has been destroyed by shoddy design and cheap manufacturing.

We need to put quality back into goods so that they have sufficient value as a material so we, our communities and our businesses can create long term economic and social value from them as we are once again are able to mend them, re-use them, remake them, transformed them, reengineer them (and their components) and eventually recycle them as food for either the biosphere or the technosphere. Critically, we must also reduce consumerism's and consumer goods' ability to act as markers of inequality, be it inequality based on economic worth, gender, age or location.

A first step in re-establishing our relationship with the goods we own as part of re-establishing our relationship with our families, friends and neighbours is to re-establish the social narratives that support community, family participation and prosperity beyond monetary worth. To do this we should first change the narrative of government. Whether in the language used in government legislation, in the language of press releases, tenders or specific social marketing communications, the language and therefore the narrative of governance needs to change. It needs to move to 'we' rather than 'I', to 'social' and 'community' from 'individual', to 'community bonds' from 'market forces'', to 'local' from 'global'. It needs to change so that a normal relationship is where communities and families are empowered by the goods and services offered by a business rather than where citizens-as-consumers are seen as essentially as market resource, existing primarily to buy stuff to keep business generating profit. This language and its ideals need to be used to reposition Scotland in the minds of its new citizens and the leaders, lent power by the peoples of Scotland.

With this change in narrative and position, the specific policies that may help build participation in society as a more satisfying, enjoyable and valuable way of spending our time, when compared to participation in a consumer society, become easier to enact. The following are some examples of what those policies might be.

Move towards fully pricing the cost of producing, maintaining and disposing of goods throughout their lifecycle. This will crucially involve fully costing the price of the pollution created across this lifecycle and must go beyond just carbon emissions (or equivalent) to include an appropriate price for the damage caused by pollutants such as environmental remediation work required to clean the land or air and the financial cost to our healthcare and welfare systems. This will act as a cost disincentive for long global supply chains and the rapid use and disposal of goods and will instead promote the local, the durable and environmentally sustainable.

Subsidies to the petrochemical industry, the car industry and other environmentally (and in some instances) socially damaging industries should instead be diverted to the building of community resources. This may include building infrastructure such as sustainable forms of transport that encourage social interaction or community facilities where sports, hobbies, the arts, political activism etc. can take place at a price cheaper than satellite TV subscription. The power to make the choices of what to build should be in the hands of communities.

We must look to reduce the power of marketing through effective marketing communication regulation including a ban on advertising to children. This may also have an additional positive effect of reducing gender inequality and stereotypes as our children are currently taught in very clear terms through marketing communications that little girls should like dolls, clothes, make up and shopping and little boys should like sport, guns and fighting.

We need to continue to explore the viability of extending marketing communications restrictions, used effectively to control for example tobacco and pharmaceuticals to other harmful substances such high fat, high sugar food stuffs and toys and must continue to restrict marketing that contributes to Scotland's agreed dysfunctional relationship with alcohol. Beyond the requirement to be legal, decent, honest and truthful, advertising should also be required not to encourage dissatisfaction with your body and sense of self.

Using these policy levers we can help reposition Scotland's relationship with material goods and with the businesses producing them. We can hopefully then rebalance the value of taking part in community, society and in the outdoors and put value back in to the material goods we buy in a way that creates opportunities for work, skills and economic and social enterprise and community prosperity.

This shift from a passive nation of consumers to an active nation of participators enables people to feel better, not worse. Taking part is good for physical health and its good for mental health. Consumption is sedentary while participation is active and consumption happens most when we feel miserable about ourselves and participation happens most when we feel good about ourselves. To be active, to engage with people, to express ourselves and to spend our time in activities which makes us feel positive emotions brings great personal and collective benefit.

So we must design for participation in the way that in the past we designed for consumption. We have to think about the activities which enhance life and have a positive effect on wellbeing. We need to expand and promote these things, make them as inexpensive as we can and make them as easy to access as we can.

There are many forms of participatory activity which are life-enriching. Many of these are as simple as socialising, meeting friends in a café or going to the pub. This needs proper high streets with proper spaces for people to meet and spend time. It means public parks in the summer and good transport links, community centres and clubs and organisations, which keep premises for social activities.

Many life-enhancing activities fall into the field of arts, culture and entertainment. So it can mean going to the cinema, a comedy club, a rock gig, a night club, the theatre, an art gallery, an opera or ballet. It might be a book reading or a discussion group, a live poetry night or an open mic comedy spot. We need to invest more in arts, culture and entertainment. We need to promote and encourage people to engage from school age onwards – becoming comfortable going into a theatre or an art gallery or a music venue should be something we develop at school by giving every pupil plenty of experience of doing this at an early age. We should put in place strategies to make the best use of existing capacity (expensive tickets mean venues may have large numbers of unfilled seats) and where there are productions in place we should seek to extend them at marginal cost to encourage greater audiences. We should encourage all our media and especially our national broadcaster to give much more emphasis to what opportunities there are.

But being a member of an audience is not the only way arts and culture create wellbeing – getting involved in amateur theatre, learning a musical instrument, doing drawing lessons, standing up and doing a routine at an open mic night, getting a band together, dancing, learning to dance or just writing for your own pleasure are all activities which improve our lives. But we need the infrastructure in place – we need places where we can do these things so we need good community facilities and the best possible access to facilities that we have (libraries, schools, arts centres and so on). We should also be building on the resources available in these venues so that it is easy to borrow a musical instrument to practice or to get materials for an art class. These comparatively inexpensive resources can make an enormous difference to how much people participate.

So does access to learning. Often what people want to do is to learn for fun or for interest. This means musical instruments and dance – but it can mean almost anything. There is a real market for inexpensive (or better still, free) availability of everything from classes in astronomy or dressmaking to interior design or car mechanics. People enjoy learning and it is a rewarding and enriching experience.

This also demonstrates just how much scope there is for being active. We should be looking at what resources people need to start dressmaking or fixing up their own car or doing more DIY round the house or baking bread or home-brewing or gardening or whatever it is they want to do. We should then aim to make sure they have easy and inexpensive or free access to those resources. For example, a community car garage where people can bring their car and use shared tools, or a room in the community centre with a few sowing machines, or decent provision of allotments.

A designed-for-profit society would see success in terms of how many DIY tools have been bought by a consumer, even if they are sitting unused in a cupboard. A designed-for-life society would have no interest in how many were bought but would care only about how many are being used. A Dutch innovation is 'share shops' where people contribute things that are useful but only needed rarely (the average use time for a battery drill from a DIY store is only about 15 minutes in the entire lifetime of the tool) and then they can borrow from the shop when they need things. This puts the tools in people's hands in a cost-free or inexpensive way and that in turn helps them be active.

Another important form of participation is sport. Fans who follow their team every weekend are highly participative. We should aim to move towards their participation in the ownership of their team. Football in particular has sometimes seen fans become nothing more than sources of income; fan-controlled football clubs are the norm in many places in the world and it is a model we can move towards in Scotland.

A designed-for-profit society would see success in terms of how many DIY tools have been bought by a consumer, even if they are sitting unused in a cupboard. A designed-for-life society would have no interest in how many were bought but would care only about how many are being used.

But to really get people participating in sport we need them to be able to get easy, local, quick access to facilities. This is the opposite direction of travel to what we have currently where local facilities have been closed down in favour of a much smaller number of bigger facilities, which are more regional than local. If we want people to be active then we must give them places to be active and provide them at a price (if not free) that makes access easy.

And we should aim to get people to participate in their nation. We have already looked at some length at how to enable people to participate properly in community politics. But our history, heritage, culture and language are also aspects of our nation that people care about and are interested in. We need to think about how we get people to engage with these things. One important step would be to prioritise the growth of domestic tourism. Scotland is a wonderful country to spend time visiting (as the many international tourists who come here will testify) but it can be expensive. The UK has some of the highest rail fares in Europe and transport costs generally which are very high by international standards. The often low levels of occupancy in the hospitality sector in Scotland can mean that prices have to be high to cover costs and sometimes there has been insufficient investment into services and training for staff. We should have a national strategy that gets people out of shopping malls at the weekend and out into their country, visiting, doing, seeing, learning. Weekend breaks or family day trips must be as attractive and as inexpensive as possible.

We should also be showcasing Scotland's culture and heritage to the world. Discussion of a Scottish Broadcasting Service has mainly been limited to considering its role in providing news and current affairs. This is important but a long way short of what we should want from a broadcaster. It is in significant part through a large and vibrant portfolio of programme-making that Scotland will define itself for itself and on the world stage. Great programme-making has no boundaries and Scotland can export high-quality TV to the world. It can also be used to stimulate a real film industry in Scotland. There has been much talk about film studios but what Scotland really needs is film commissions, people paying for films to be made. A national broadcaster should invest heavily in film-making, partly because films are an important way to show Scotland to the world but also because film-making is one of the best ways to sustain the entire arts community – from musicians and set designers to writers, actors and the many film trades.

We can design our nation for life, for participation, for happiness and wellbeing. But we need active citizens. So let us end where so much begins; at school. For too long we have seen schooling as a process of assessment. The purpose of school (in conflict-driven, Me-First politics) is seen as a means of separating children into categories – academic or non-academic, future leaders or future losers, the bright and the not-bright. The demand of universities to have ways of assessing the academic potential of candidates has fuelled this, as has a league table culture which pits not just pupil against pupil but school against school in a 'survival of the fittest' battle. The pressure on pupils to memorise 'correct' answers and to learn the rules of passing the exam game is intense. It is therefore less surprising than it should be that a recent World Health Organisation survey found that British children are the least happy in the world.

There are four identified goals of education. Learning to know is about how pupils become able to gather and use information. Learning to do is about practical skills. Learning to be is about discovering who they are and what is important to them. Learning to live together is about how to create positive social relationships. We must take this full range of child development more seriously. It is not the assessment of a child that we should care about more but the attainment – do they know more, understand better, feel more sure about themselves, act positively towards others? We should see the knowledge that makes someone a good citizen prioritised every bit as much as the knowledge that makes someone a good employee.

So we need to make schools places which, above all other aims, produce happy, rounded, intelligent, creative and curious citizens. We need to think not just in terms of the nature of the curriculum but in terms of the nature of how children learn. And we need to value a much wider range of attainment than simply 'can they read, can they write, can they count?'. Knowledge of the history of ideas, the arts movements, the science of our bodies, our past and the world around us are critical in creating rounded citizens.

A Common Weal Scotland is one which is designed for life. It is a nation that enhances the sense of happiness, fulfilment and wellbeing of its citizens.

Epilogue

Inequality, low rates of investment, poor economic performance and poverty - you may have been told that these are so complicated that no-one really knows how to start to tackle them. Hopefully you no longer believe that. Hopefully you can see a realistic path to a future where we have successfully tackled these problems, just as they have been successful at tackling them in other countries.

What might we need to get there? There is a lot in Common Weal that can be done with Scotland's existing powers, but there is much that can't. To make a serious start we need powers. These would include borrowing powers, powers over welfare policy, workplace regulation, ownership of assets (such as the National Grid) and tax powers (though basic rate income tax is not the main tax power required). It would also be helpful to have powers such as competitions policy, banking regulation and wage policy. And foriegn policy is obviously key to some of it. So it is for you to decide the best way to get those powers.

Then we need a politics which is capable of delivering this kind of change. We need political parties which will take on vested interests and be willing to challenge the Me-First narratives which are too often taken as fact. We need political parties which have a real vision for transformation. And we need political parties which embrace democracy and empower citizens to challenge political power - even if it is sometimes uncomfortable. So it is for you to choose and shape those political parties.

Then we need a lively, energised, empowered community right across Scotland which talks about and campaigns for a better future and a genuinely engaged population which believes politics to be something that they can influence and change.

Power, will and leadership; we have everything else we need to build a Common Weal Scotland. Can we find these things?

The prize if we can is enormous. Finally, after generations in which the hope of real change was either missing or an illusion, we may genuinely be ready to build a better nation.

And so, in the end, it is up to you. Is the Scotland you read about in these pages the Scotland where you want to live? Then stop waiting for someone else to give you it and take it for yourself.

Only then can we end Me-First politics. Only then can we have a Scotland that really does put all of us first.

List of Common Weal Reports

Using Our Buying Power to Benefit Scotland
Feb 2012
Public procurement
and economics development

The Silent Crisis
May 2012
Local democracy

No Need to Be Afraid
Oct 2012
National security, human security
and defence

The Case for Universalism
Dec 2012
Universalism and public services

Not By The People
Feb 2013
Political influence and lobbying

The Mismanagement of Britain
Apr 2103
Economic management

The Dysfunctional UK Economy
May 2013
Economic management

No More Excuses
Aug 2013
Poverty and equality

Economic Policy Options for an Independent Scotland
Sep 2013
Economic development

Investing in the Good Society
Sep 2013
Tax and public finance

Repossessing the Future
Sep 2013
Energy

Government By The People
Oct 2013
Participatory democracy

Working Together
Nov 2013
Industrial democracy

Scotland and International Trade Organisations
Jan 2014
International trade

The Future of the Energy Storage Industry in Scotland
Jan 2014
Energy storage

A Common Weal Education
Feb 2014
Education

In Place of Anxiety
Mar 2014
Welfare and social security

Occupational Health and Safety
in Scotland
Mar 2014
Health and safety

Social Justice, the Common Weal
and Children and Young People
in Scotland
Apr 2014
Participatory democracy
and children

Time for Life
Apr 2014
Working hours

An Atlas of Productivity
May 2014
Economic geography

Towards and Industrial Policy
for Scotland
Jun 2014
Economic development

An Investment Plan for Scotland
Jun 2014
Finance and investment

Housing for the Common Weal
Jun 2014
Housing

Banking on Trust
Jun 2014
Community banking

Forthcoming Reports:

Citizen's Income
Human rights
Media
21 Possible Industries
Language and Legislation
Digital Comms and Postal Service
Transport
Land Reform
Food Sovereignty
Town centres and planning
Community regeneration
Sport
Environmental protection
Community Development
Constitution
Health
Gender
Pensions
Deconsumerisation
Arts and Culture
Tourism
Justice and policing
Civil Service and institutions
Heritage, culture, language

All of the reports can be found
at www.reidfoundation.org
and on allofusfirst.org where
there is ongoing discussion of
Common Weal.